T0319182

I AM NALA

NalaFem

I AM NALA

PUBLISHED BY NALA FEMINIST COLLECTIVE

Edited by:

Managing Editor

Dr. Novuyo Tshuma

Editors

Ms. Amina Alaoui Soulimani

Dr. Syeda Re'em Hussain

Ms. Rahel Weldeab Sebhatu

Ms. Soraya Addi

NalaFem

Funded by Rockefeller Foundation

ISBN: 978-9914-741-48-3

Nala Feminist Collective
P.O. Box 258-00621
Nairobi
Kenya

NalaFem

TABLE OF CONTENTS

NalaFem

Foreword

Africa's women for Africa's renewal.

"Women' rights are human's rights" was the signature quote from Hilary Clinton and was a clarion call to address female right. The Convention on the Elimination of All Forms of Discrimination against Women (CEDAW) conference in Beijing in 1995 was indeed a landmark conference.

Now that CEDAW is over twenty-five years old, it will be good as African women to go down memory lane and take stock of progress and ask ourselves to what extent the promised reforms have been implemented. We must also examine why progress has been limited in many countries and we need to seek ways to overcome the obstacles.

There is no doubt that some improvements have been made as moves have been made to implement the recommendations made at the CEDAW conference. There have been attempts made towards the development of new policies and guidelines and the creation of networks of gender experts. Yet in spite of these efforts, one gets the impression—to use the famous Moonshot moment—that Men have gone to the moon and back while Women are still in the starting block with a society still trying to sensitise itself on the unacceptable marginalisation of women. Women are slowly coming to terms with a society that has been and is still depriving her of her rights—constitutionally or otherwise.

In Africa, women have made important strides especially in the political arena—at least for some countries and regions. The African Union has made a special effort to promote gender parity within a few of its bodies. African women have lobbied hard to ensure that many countries ratify CEDAW or better known in UN language as the International Bill of Rights for Women.

Unfortunately, obstacles persist and issues like poverty reduction strategies still do not take into account differences in income and power between men and women, hampering efforts to finance programmes that reduce inequality. In addition, the majority of African women are still being denied education and employment, still face violence, political and economic inequality, and have limited opportunities in trade, industry, and government. Poverty still has a woman's face because women generally feel that the instruments their respective governments have signed have failed to be translated into positive changes in their daily lives.

Compounding the situation are setbacks such as the HIV/AIDS pandemic that is destroying the health of more women than men in Africa, eroding some of the development gains women had attained. Over twenty-five years after Beijing, African women are much poorer. More often than not, men are more likely to find a job and enterprises run by men have easier access to support from institutions such as banks.

In Africa, women have made important strides especially in the political arena—at least for some countries and regions. The African Union has made a special effort to promote gender parity within a few of its bodies.

African women have lobbied hard to ensure that many countries ratify CEDAW or better known in UN language as the International Bill of Rights for Women.

Perhaps the most inhibiting factor is that women in Africa continue to be denied an education, often the only ticket out of poverty. Disparities between girls and boys start in primary school and the differences widen through the entire educational system. In total enrollment in primary education, Africa registered the highest relative increase among regions during the last decade. But given the low proportion of girls being enrolled, the continent is still far from the goal of attaining intake parity. Policies specifically targeting girls were responsible for considerable improvements in many African countries, thanks also to policies sensitising parents through the media, reducing school fees, and providing a modicum infrastructure such as toilets for girls in public primary schools in rural areas.

By the time children go through high school and reach college, the gender gap becomes even wider and is revealed through the low participation of women especially in STEM and other technical fields.

It is acknowledged that to enable women to escape poverty, development policies should place more emphasis on their contributions to the economy. Even though women make up a significant proportion of the economically active population, their contribution is not fully recorded because they are mainly engaged in family farming or in the informal sector. In other cases, what they do, such as household work, is not considered an economic activity.

In agriculture, sub-Saharan Africa's most vital economic sector, women contribute 60–80 per cent of labour in food production, both for household consumption and for sale. But while they do most of the work, they lack access to markets and credit.

In spite of all the challenges, women in some African countries have moved into positions of political influence with countries like Rwanda leading the way in terms of representation of women leadership at the political level where the world average is just fifteen per cent. Yet it is clear that the presence of women in parliament has made a difference in the adoption of gender-sensitive policies. The quota system is more than needed if legislations like the legalising abortion, countering domestic violence, family law, and ensuring child support are to be voted in.

It is thus clear that in global debates, women's issues should not be made simplistic or reduced to a single denominator. Women's issues, from the girl child all the way up to womanhood, must be all encompassing and must be protected from violence and harmful practices. Countries must put in place basic strategies to lift women out of poverty and halt the spread of diseases.

Empowerment of women should not be confined to a narrow range of sectors within countries but should also ensure the equal participation of women in fast-moving global processes, because equality is still not a reality.

Dr. Ameenah Gurib-Fakim
Former President of Mauritius

Foreword

More than twenty-five years ago, the global community adopted progressive blueprints for gender equality and social justice at the International Conference on Population and Development in Cairo in 1994 and the Fourth World Conference on Women in Beijing in 1995.

Those landmark consensus documents, reinforced during the Nairobi Summit on ICPD25 and the Generation Equality Forum commemorating Beijing+25, expressed the conviction that women and girls belong squarely at the centre of development policy and decision making.

Their message was simple—people first, with priority attention to women and girls. Over the past two decades we have made remarkable gains. Fewer women die in pregnancy and childbirth. More women are using modern contraception. More girls are in school. We are beginning to turn the tide against harmful practices such as child marriage and female genital mutilation. Yet for far too many women and girls, the world we envisioned in Cairo and Beijing is still far from reality. Nearly half the world's women still cannot make their own decisions about whether to have sex, use contraception or seek healthcare. No country has yet achieved gender equality, and many of the targets under Sustainable Development Goal 5 are far from being met. This should outrage us all.

As we continue our march for equality, and for reproductive health, rights and justice for all, collections such as this one, documenting the stories of feminist leaders, thinkers, and doers, offer hope and inspiration for our collective journey.

NalaFem

History shows us that social movements, especially feminist movements, can bring about transformative change. They have played an instrumental role in establishing and advancing sexual and reproductive health and rights over the years. The Nala Feminist Collective personifies that fierce and unwavering commitment.

UNFPA is committed to working together with and for social movements, particularly those amplifying the voices of groups often left out or left behind. Together, we can accelerate human rights-based, gender-transformative, people-centered sustainable development and peace. We know from experience that solidarity, through partnerships and alliances, can rapidly improve the well-being of women and girls, transform families and societies, and accelerate global development. It can change the world.

Dr. Natalia Kanem
Executive Director, United Nations Population Fund (UNFPA)

Introduction

Change that transforms institutions, ideologies and systems requires collective and complementary influence work where decision-makers are persuaded, embarrassed into and even forced to make decisions in the favour of women and girls and those who are forced to the margins based on gender, race, age, ability, class and other factors. Collectives are needed to harness the most powerful and compelling ideas to influence change proactively. Collective action through coalition work is central to movement building approaches. Advocacy as part of coalitions and support for collective action by various feminist formations is key to building movements and creating systemic change. That is why Nala's role and influence is in this ecosystem for social change.

Nala Feminist Collective (NalaFEM) is a Pan-African front of feminist leaders with a mission to Foster, Enable and Mobilize (FEM) women and girls from Africa and the Diaspora. We use multi-track diplomacy, advocacy & communications to bridge the gap between policy & implementation, intergovernmental & grassroots as well as generational spaces. This platform emerged in 2020 from the Africa Young Women Beijing+25 Manifesto (B+25 Manifesto) developed in consultation with 1500 African youth from 44 countries and over 30 partners under the mandate of Ms. Aya Chebbi as the African Union Special Envoy on Youth .

The B+25 Manifesto is a groundbreaking feminist political document that sets out critical issues of concern for young women of Africa and makes demands for addressing them.

The Manifesto is the result of five Regional Barazas that convened over 1500 young people from across 44 African countries and over 30 partners from 12 - 30 October 12 2020. The B+25 Manifesto was handed over during Africa Young Women Beijing+25 High-Level Intergenerational Dialogue on 25 November 2020, to Amb. Delphine O (Secretary General of the Generation Equality Forum), H.E. Bineta Diop (African Union Special Envoy on Women, Peace and Security), and Phumzile Mlambo-Ngucka (Executive Director of UN Women). The Manifesto therefore provides a platform of a common set of demands for the achievement of gender equity for Agenda 2063 and Agenda 2030.

These engagements birthed Nalafem which led a mobilization campaign between April and May 2021 advocating for African feminists' voices at the Generation Equality Forums (GEF), the Action Coalitions which led to collecting 10.360 signatures of B+25 Manifesto from over 105 countries. NalaFEM's efforts in collaboration with partners and youth activists succeeded to include 8 out of the 10 demands into Action Coalitions and Women, Peace and Security and Humanitarian Action Compact. The 10 Demands are namely: Economic Justice; Criminalize Gender-Based Violence; End Gender-Based Discrimination; Access to Justice and Protection; Sexual and Reproductive Health and Rights; Mental Health and Well-Being, Inclusive; Equitable and Quality Education; Digital Justice; Silencing the Guns; and Intergenerational Co-Leadership.

Following the successful campaign, NalaFEM was officially launched during the Generation Equality Forum in Paris on 1st July 2021.

Bringing the Action Coalitions closer to young feminists, was the priority of NalaFEM for GEF. Following the Paris forum, NalaFEM partnered with youth organizations to convene six Intergenerational Accountability Dialogues in order to support the implementation of the Action Coalitions commitments at national levels, and engage African women and girls in the 5-year journey of accountability on the international community's commitment of USD40 billion.

The collective is steered by Nala Council which consists of seventeen women leaders under the age of forty who are among the youngest and boldest women in politics and activism. Each council member is fiercely advocating for one of the ten demands of B+25 manifesto, one of the seventeen sustainable development goals of Agenda 2030 and one of the seven aspirations of Agenda 2063.

As we publish this book Nala council meets for the annual retreat to adopt a five year strategy with five flagship projects that include Nala Academy, Nala Fund, GEF Index, Nala Summit and Awards as well as the 100 Intergenerational Accountability Dialogues.

Nala is not an NGO (Non Governmental Organisation) but rather a platform and coalition of feminists to set the agenda, unlock the power of women and girls as well as hold leaders accountable to their GEF commitments. With strategic partnerships and the generous support of diverse stakeholders, we are able to deliver our mission including this self-published advocacy book.

This project is powered by Afresist Centre, the convening organization of the Nala Feminist Collective.

Editorial Note

by Dr. Novuyo Tshuma

The seven stories in this compilation are a testimony to an Africa that is alive and vibrant and whose future brims with brilliance and promise. Working with the team of editors on these brave, brilliant, and inspiring stories, I often found myself overcome with awe, gratitude, and pride at the work these seven incredible women do and continue to do. I am proud to be part of the African continent and the African Diaspora. We have overcome so much. Readers from all corners of the world will feel this immense pride and inspiration, too. For Africa is in and of the world.

Here you will meet women in their twenties and thirties who have broken new ground and attained many firsts in their respective fields, in this way paving way for African women and girls and hence women and girls everywhere. You will meet the founder of NalaFEM, Ms. Aya Chebbi, who served as the first ever African Union Special Envoy on Youth and the youngest diplomat at the African Union Commission Chairperson's Cabinet. Ms. Chebbi takes us through her journey growing up in Tunisia, forging her own path and finding her powerful, radical voice that has resonated on the streets and in boardrooms in over eighty countries around the world. From the streets of protest during Tunisia's Revolution of Dignity in 2010-2011 to engaging Presidents and World Leaders in diplomatic boardrooms, Ms. Chebbi's courage, vulnerability and sense of purpose awakens us to the fact that a Pan-Africanism that excludes women is not a true Pan-Africanism at all. Her story inspires us to find our radical selves and claim our freedom.

You will meet Ms. Bogolo Joy Kenewendo, a global economist and the former Minister of Investment, Trade and Industry of Botswana. At age thirty-one, she became the youngest Cabinet Minister in Africa and the youngest Minister in Botswana's history during her tenure. Ms. Kenewendo takes us through her journey growing up in Motopi Village in Botswana and her early advocacy helping the poor and the disenfranchised in her community, to her landmark swearing into the Botswana Ministerial Cabinet at age thirty-one. She imparts invaluable lessons learned throughout her trail-blazing journey and offers indispensable insights on Africa, policy, the economy, and women's leadership and empowerment. Told in an intimate and commanding voice, her incredible journey of purpose empowers and inspires African women and girls everywhere.

You will meet Ms. Martine Kessy Ekomo Soignet, who is the founder of Peace and Development Watch Central African Republic and who in 2016 was appointed by the Secretary-General of the United Nations as an expert for the Progress Study on the Youth, Peace and Security Agenda. Ms. Soignet takes us through her experiences living through war as a child in the Central African Republic, her awakening to the world's injustices and her determination to do something about it, as well as her incredible journey finding her voice as an advocate for youth and peace on the African Continent and beyond. With grace and power, Ms Soignet invites us all to "plant seeds of hope" and flourish like the Adansonia Digitata, the magnificent African Baobab tree.

You will meet Ms. Oluwaseun Ayodeji Osowobi, a national advocate for survivors of gender and sexual-based violence in Nigeria and founder of the Stand to End Rape Initiative (STER). In 2019, Ms. Osowobi helped establish Nigeria's first national Sex Offenders Register. She takes us through her experiences growing up in the southern part of Nigeria and, with a keen and caring eye for the society around her, narrates the formative experiences that led to her ground-breaking activism and, ultimately, a seminal journey that has led to social and systemic change in Nigeria. This moving and empowering narrative reminds us that we can all rise up and effect change in our societies and in this way become the heroines of our own stories.

You will meet Ms. Rosebell Kagumire, a writer, editor and Pan-African feminist activist who works at the intersection of media, gender, and development. In chronicling Uganda's struggle to attain independence and define its freedom, Ms. Kagumire takes us through an intergenerational family tale of lives lived and hopes dreamed. She explores the legacy of colonial education and the boarding school system and its poignant effects on young girls on the cusp of adolescence. Told in both intimate and broad strokes, Ms. Kagumire deftly paints for us the breaking up of families and the disruption of indigenous teachings that are the social fabric of many African societies and, coupled with this, the colonial legacies of the boarding school system that continue to make permissible the violation of girls' bodies. This poignant story is a rallying cry for the recognition of girls everywhere and a reform of Africa's colonial education systems.

You will meet Ms. Rose Wachuka Macharia, the first female and youngest Chief of Staff to the Chief Justice and President of the Supreme Court of Kenya Hon. Justice Martha K. Koome, EBS. Ms. Macharia takes us through her journey growing up in a family of brilliant and strong-willed women whose excellence and trajectory was hampered by the limits placed on them by society. In writing that is intimate, contemplative, and intellectually and emotionally moving, Ms. Macharia's commitment to fight for the freedom of women and girls and her brilliant work to reform Kenya's legal system inspire a love for liberty and a feminist awakening. In fighting for the freedom of women and girls, she fights for freedom for us all.

You will meet Ms. Yasmine Ouirhrane, who is co-founder of We Belong, a platform and podcast that amplifies the voice of the New Daughters of Europe, immigrant descents. Ms. Ouirhrane takes us through her experiences of social discrimination as an immigrant growing up in Italy and her own spatial journey of migration from Italy to France at the age of fifteen. She has been volunteering in the underprivileged neighborhoods of France to foster social inclusion since the age of sixteen. Ms. Ouirhrane's inspiring journey chronicles the all too familiar experiences of social exclusion and discrimination faced by many immigrants in Europe and beyond. Told in a powerful and moving voice, her journey of self-reclamation and her powerful advocacy for immigrant youth in spaces where they are excluded, unheard and unseen, empowers us to harness difference and diversity as essential attributes that enrich our lives and strengthen our societies.

These seven stories narrate powerful and empowering journeys of becoming and overcoming. The women in this anthology are deeply attuned to the challenges and hardships faced by women and girls on the African continent and in the Diaspora. They do not shy away from speaking about these hardships, offering up vulnerable stories that are emblematic of the ongoing disregard of women and girls in Africa and elsewhere. Triumphantly, these hardships fuel these inspiring women to claim their right to humanity, in this way effecting change in their societies and trailblazing a path for women and girls in Africa and beyond. Ultimately, these are triumphant stories of change and agency. They pave the way for future generations and make possible for us what was previously thought impossible. We thank the women of NalaFEM for their groundbreaking work and their ongoing contributions. Siyabonga!

CHAPTER ONE

Your Power is Your Radical Self. Find it
by Aya Chebbi

"I am Nala
because I found power in my voice"

Tasfih - the ritual

The old lady made cuts on my left knee seven times until they. bled, then she dipped seven raisins in my fresh blood and forced me to eat them. The taste of blood mixed with the sweetness of raisins still remains in my mouth to this day. My female cousins and I went through the same ritual that day called " تصفيح tasfih" or "the locker", and we were told to repeat the words "*I'm a wall and he's a thread. Blood from my knee, close my little hole*".

What could I do but cry!
As a young girl, I was powerless.
Fighting it would have been in vain, anyway.

They said the spell would be lifted on the day of my wedding. I had barely reached puberty, yet I was already learning how things for young women *should* be.

I grew up in a very conservative Muslim family. We lived in a small village called Dahmani on the Tunisian-Algerian border. At the age of nine, I had to go through tasfih like all the girls in my family, generation after generation. The mystical ritual of tasfih is practiced mainly in rural Tunisia, Morocco, and Algeria. It is believed the execution of the ritual protects girls from sexual contact by preventing sexual intercourse, whether it is wanted or unwanted, desired or forced. In this way, it guarantees their virginity until marriage.

To lift the spell, one performs the same ritual of tasfih, this time repeating, "He is a wall, I am a thread."

In this way, one reverses the formula that sealed one's virginity and is able to offer it to one's husband. Not much was explained to me that hot summer afternoon besides the warning that no one was to touch me except my future husband at my wedding.

Going through the ritual at age nine was the start of a long-term trauma for me. Until the age of thirty, I was haunted by vivid memories of the cuts and the subsequent bleeding. I found I wasn't able to have sexual intimacy in relationships because tasfih created an illusion in my mind that I was armoured.

There was no time for me to heal in a society that does not consider trauma healing a necessity for children's growth, let alone girls. So, we continue to carry the weight of the damage done to our minds long after our skin has scarred.

A few weeks after my first ritual of tasfih, it was put to the test.

I was walking to school one rainy morning when my umbrella broke. I found refuge in a nearby cemetery, not far from our house. I pressed myself into a wall, trying to shelter from the rain. A long shadow crept up behind me. I turned to find a young man carrying an umbrella.

"Kiss me,' he said, 'and I'll protect you from the rain."

I did not understand what he meant by "kissing," but I was frightened by the malice on his face. I started crying. He put a hand over my mouth and dragged me inside the cemetery. I do not want to recall the rest.

It felt like I had entered into a coma where I could only hear my voice screaming inside my head. I closed my eyes and held myself with my arms.

Then, gathering all the mental and physical strength my little body had, I opened my eyes. Eventually, I managed to escape. I ran home, soaked from the rain and my tears.

Wasn't tasfih supposed to protect me? This magical practice performed by making young girls bleed to shield their virginity proved at this very moment to be the manifestation of patriarchy. According to UN Women statistics, one in three women experience sexual assault in their lifetime. This doesn't include the baseline submission expected of women and girls, who are forced to engage in unwanted sexual behaviour. As a result of the violence perpetuated by patriarchy, we walk around with these sexual wounds, covered in sexual shaming and guilt and self-criticism.

Not many people know about tasfih and its gendered cultural legacy in the Maghreb region. It is but one of many forms of repressing women's sexuality. A worse practice is Female Genital Mutilation (FGM) which involves partial or total removal of the external female genitalia, or other injury to the female genital organs for non-medical reasons. Two hundred million girls have been subjected to the practice already, with one hundred and twenty-five million of them in Africa. Female genital mutilation not only has psychological implications like tasfih but also medical complications, from severe pain to prolonged bleeding, infection, infertility, increased risk of HIV transmission, and even death. Hence, the girls subjected to this practice are physically and mentally destroyed.

I failed to escape the social belief of tasfih that is deeply entrenched in many Tunisian women's consciousness. Despite the fact that I oppose this practice, to date my mother believes I am "protected," something she is proud of. She thinks it was the right thing to do.

Even though tasfih has become a rare practice, it still remains popular in many families, including families in my village Dahmani, as a form of protection against growing sexual freedom in Tunisia.

After crying the night after I escaped from the man at the cemetery, I realised that being a girl under patriarchy meant my story was told for me by others before I could even articulate it. The tasfih spell "locks" me in childhood and "unlocks" me decades later in preparation for my wedding night.

This realisation provoked a reflection of my girlhood and womanhood in general; I began to examine the way female bodies are represented and to question my place as a woman in relationships, in family settings, and in society. Torn between tradition and a deep need for emancipation, I started to challenge the centrality of marriage as a destination and the societal belief that the most worthy part of me is *my hymen*, a thin piece of tissue.

We have an Arabic phrase that is often used in newspapers and films: "افقدها أغلى ماعندها"— "He made her lose her most precious thing." Virginity is treated as the most sacred, valuable thing a woman can have, as if my brain, my arms, or my fingers are not equally precious. Society's mission, then, becomes "unlocking" a woman's virginity instead of unlocking her potential.

This obsession with a girl's sexual life, and the act of suppressing female sexual desires, are astonishing. Although no religious scriptures require these harmful practices, religion is used to justify them as acts that are directly linked to a family's "honor." Where I grew up, discourses on culture and religion continue to be used to justify and legitimise the violence practiced against women. This needs to stop. I know one day, I will play a role in ending it.

Feminist Father

When I got my period, they said,
"Don't wear shorts, learn how to cook, don't cross your legs..."
My mum asked, "When are you getting married?"
My dad asked, "When are you getting your degree?"
At least, he saw me, before I saw myself.

I grew up as an only child. My father, a retired Colonel Major who served forty-two years and eight days in the Tunisian Armed Forces, imbued in me a strong sense of self-worth and a conviction that I deserve the same chances in life as anyone else. He used his privilege as a man, as the "head of the family," to pave the way for me to be and become. He provided protection for the consequences of my "radical" actions in the perception of relatives, neighbors, and our community.

Regardless of how deep our disagreements could be, my right to make my own choices was always guaranteed. He nurtured my courage to be bold. It really takes a lot of courage in our societies as young women to be bold, to speak up. It takes courage every day to reveal our fullest truth to the world and to lead the battle for ourselves.

He is about 5 ft. 7, bald and with an extremely tough aura, but is actually the funniest personality out of the military barracks. He has unique light grey eyes and a beautiful smile with gappy teeth. His support has allowed me to explore all facets of who I am far from who I should be.

When I think of a feminist man, I think of my father.
I felt I had to choose to either rebel and liberate myself or submit to imposed powerlessness.

I did not want to be social property, a second-class citizen with no control over my sexuality, my political being, my economic power, and my contributions to society.

Liberation starts as a mindset. Having a supportive father opened up possibilities for me to rebel.

I felt empowered to be radical.

Mosaic Life

I also had privileges. Because of my dad's line of work, which required constant moving, I discovered the complexity and disparities in our country.

We had to move as a family to a different city every two to four years. That meant a new town and a new school. We travelled from the northmost to the southmost parts of Tunisia. I attended eight different schools. Living in the underdeveloped southern and central parts of Tunisia gave me a sense of the social marginalisation and poverty in the country. I've also seen the mosaic of Tunisia, its more opulent parts. These multi-cultural facets fed me in ways my education could not.

When I was thirteen and living in a southern city called Medenine, I visited a small town called Matmata where I found out about "Tamazight." I thought people were speaking with a southern accent I couldn't understand, but the children I played with told me Tamazight is our language. It is the native language of the indigenous people of North Africa, our people. It is unfortunate that our dense history of three thousand years is manipulatively summed up in terms as general as, "Tunisia's geopolitical location was a crossroad of civilizations."

We are taught that by the end of the nineteenth century, Tunisians comprised Moors, Turks, Jews, Andalusians, Arabs, and various sorts of Europeans. However, we are not taught about the original population. Learning about Tamazight made me curious about my identity within the diversity I experienced due to my nomadic family life.

I started to be more aware of the privileges I was born with versus the privileges I had acquired.

The way I wanted myself to be noticed in every school was by being top of the class and by getting the attention of the most popular boy in the school. Even though these might seem like contradictory behaviors, they were both signs of empowerment; knowing what I wanted and being a goal getter.

In high school I was bullied for my curly hair being a "mess." I was told over and over again, "شعرك كلمصلحة"— "your hair is like a broom." So, I kept it short, very short. Next, I was called a tomboy because of my short hair, so I let it grow longer and straightened it. My mom would wrap it every night in long tights for it to be perfectly in shape for the next day.

I was also bullied for my thick glasses, which I had worn since third grade and which my peers called "قاع دبوزة"— "the bottom of the bottle." At least this was an object I could change every other year. Sometimes, I would break my glasses on purpose so I could have them changed.

I was also bullied for my gap teeth, which we did not have enough money to "fix." I was told a gap between the front teeth was not a "typical standard of beauty," but deep down, I actually liked my gap because my father has an even larger one between his teeth. I loved looking like him and for everyone to notice that I was his daughter.

I smile at these memories when I look at Barbados' eighth Prime Minister and first female Prime Minister, Mia Amor Mottley, delivering her powerful speech at the 26th United Nations Climate Change Conference (COP26) with her open, effortless, gap-toothed smile.

Today, increasingly, girls are more likely to be bullied than boys. For girls, the most common form of bullying is name calling, appearance-based taunting, and social exclusion. Perhaps that's why as a girl, I tried to "fit in," to change my looks, lose weight or isolate myself. Attempting to fit in leads to a sense of worthlessness, which is dangerous.

Just as in my childhood, my teenage body was a battlefield for others to assess or mock according to their own opinions, criteria, and internalised colonial narrative.

During my adolescence, it was so important to hear my dad's affirmation of "my worth." He would sit and listen to me reciting my poetry attempts. He would reward me with my favorite chocolate for every excellent grade I got. He encouraged me to play sports and even Karate so as to be able to "kick the boy's ass when he deserves it," as he would say.

Every girl needs someone like my father, a figure to trust, ask, listen to, and look up to; someone who can remind you that no one else can determine your worth but yourself.

Public Space

When I turned eighteen, my father left for the United Nations' military Blue Helmets Peacekeeping Mission in the Democratic Republic of Congo. It was the year I graduated from high school and got my bacalaureat.

I felt I had to face the world alone.

I had to learn to fly on my own and protect myself.

Public spaces are where I struggled the most to fend for myself. I was regularly touched against my will in public transportation. One day, on a sunny winter afternoon, a short man in his early thirties stood behind me in a very crowded Tunis Metro and masturbated in between stations. I did not realise what had happened until I'd left the metro only to find my whole back was wet. I stood there, terrified.

The public space in Tunisia has overwhelmingly been male dominated, often reducing women to objects of struggle, using Islam as a pretext for safeguarding Tunisia's culture and morals after decades of colonial rule. Public spaces are a symbol of gender segregation. For instance, the majority of coffee houses are for men only. I have often been told to pass by *men-only* cafes with my head down.

During my dad's absence, I struggled in public spaces and found myself letting others decide my life for me. When my eldest uncle decided I should attend an engineering school at École Préparatoire d'Ingénieurs and follow in his son's footsteps, I went to that school, even though I wanted to study pharmacy. I failed the first semester, and by the third semester I'd dropped out of university altogether. I realised how fragile I was without my "protector." Having always been top of my class, this academic failure shoved me into a deep depression.

"I am a school dropout," I told myself, "Not because it's a gap year to travel the world or that I can't afford to attend a public university, but simply because I failed."

I did not want to go back to school. I wanted to just find a job and go about my days. After a tough summer spent locked up in my room, it was again my father who held my hand and said, "Try again, get the degree, then do whatever you want."

I visited about four universities in different cities in Tunisia looking for whatever college would enroll me. I integrated into the University Tunis El Manar and switched from science to the humanities to study International Relations, which I excelled in with my scientific background. I was top of my class again.

This success boosted my confidence and awakened my need to fight and not ever give up again. I spent the four years at Institut Supérieur des Sciences Humaines de Tunis in "warrior mode," probably needing to prove something. Every time I heard, "you can't do it," a fire inside me would light up and I would put all my energy in pursuing that "it" they said I could not do.

At university, I filled my time with purpose. I volunteered in every organisation I knew, created clubs where there weren't any, taught extracurricular classes in high schools during the weekends, learned sign language, ran workshops for kids fighting cancer at the Children's Hospital Bab Saadoun, spent summers in camps training children with disabilities, spent Eid al-Fitr at SOS, and Ramadan at Iftar tables.

Volunteerism taught me not to think only about myself or my father's good health, but to also think about the jobless, the illiterate, the poor, and the sick in my community.

For, you see, I was never a rebel in search of superficial popularity, nor was I a warrior seeking an easy win. In a Tunisia that was stagnating in the injustices I had seen since childhood, I was in pursuit of a cause.

I think my first leadership attempts were the hardest because my responsibilities included being responsible for children while I was still "a child" myself. I took the lead and organised multiple events for children at orphanages, hospitals, and integration centers. Putting a smile on these kids' faces gave me a definition of who I should be every day; serving others, uplifting others, inspiring others.

Revolution of Dignity

During my graduation year, the revolution happened... I found myself ready to be fully involved in the change making.

"Game Over! Game Over!"

The voice of freedom was rising from different corners in Tunis, mixed with pain and bravery.

Thousands of people poured in from different directions, filling every stretch of Habib Bourguiba Avenue. The café-lined street turned into a scene of civil resistance.

Young women. Unemployed graduates. Journalists. Doctors. Lawyers. Students. Some climbed the walls of the Interior Ministry, a site of torture reports for years. I dropped Tunisia's red and white flag on my back and joined the chanting.

"No fear, no horror! The street belongs to the people!"

I was angry and fearless.

Hundreds of placards were lifted above our heads with different colours and the boldly inscribed message, "Ben Ali Dégage!"—Ben Ali Leave! We held our message as high as our arms would allow, while walking through thick clouds of tear gas and black smoke.

"*Leave! Leave!*" we shouted.

Police. Teargas. Shooting. Citizens. Screaming. Running. Silence. The voice of freedom slowly returned, louder and more powerful, but peaceful. The teargas was not going to stop us this time. This time, the collective steps were walking forward with a harmonious and united voice.

"*The people demand the overthrow of the regime!*"

The world stood in anticipation as we chanted with tears and cried with smiles. These were moments of freedom, of dignity. I had long known that every revolution is driven by youth, but I did not know I would be taking part in one. The revolution helped me experience how the power of the people is more powerful than the people in power.

Protest turned into celebration as news started filling our social media feeds and the streets that Friday night: President Zine El Abdine Ben Ali (ZABA) had resigned and fled. His twenty-three-year dictatorship—the only government I had known my entire life —was over.

When I remember January 14th, 2011, I remember the noise. I remember the silence. I remember the words of the Tunisian poet, Abu Al Kacem Chebbi, echoing in my head: "You were born unbound like the shadow of the breeze, and free like the light of the dawn in its sky."

Riots had broken out after Mohamed Bouazizi, a twenty-six-year-old street vendor, self-immolated to protest the injustice he experienced in his small town of Sidi Bouzid on December 17, 2010.

The uprising resulted from years of militantism, especially during the Revolt of Gafsa Mining basin of 2008.

We were preparing to sit for final exams that January when, because of increasing protests, ZABA decided to shut down public schools and universities. Freed from the classroom during the shutdown, we could focus on organising and protesting.

I knew that the dangers of protesting in the streets included being subjected to indiscriminate teargas and police violence. State news media warned repeatedly that police would shoot. But I also knew the alternative to confronting the government was worse: the state of *waithood*. Without change, my generation would have been condemned to perpetual waiting: waiting for employment, for political inclusion, for social justice, and much more. So, I decided to go out on the streets and join the resistance.

As an International Relations student, I was constantly challenging George Orwell's 1984 totalitarian regime outside the classroom. I found myself as a protester, photographer, blogger, documenter, elections observer, humanitarian, campaigner, organiser, and everything I did not think I could be. My passion for Freedom was born as my beloved homeland was being reborn into the second republic. The "radical" in me matured into a political voice, an activist looking for true liberation that could finally manifest during the revolution in ways I did not think possible.

Being part of the revolution made me believe that change can happen and that we, young women, are at the forefront. It was a moment of fearlessness. Nothing has seemed impossible to me ever since. Young women like myself took to the streets, unafraid to die for freedom. We left the walls of Facebook to tag the brick and concrete walls. A strong sense of belonging and unity emerged with the uprising because the fear had vanished. In all honesty, there would always be fear, fear of the unknown, fear for our life.

Our choice, however, resides in the point at which we either let the fear control us or we act beyond that fear. I think the revolution gave me that sense of protection again: anyone who would harass me in a protest would have to deal with the one hundred women beside me. I have since understood that everything I had been through was leading me to the fall of Ben Ali.

Soon after ZABA left, the world felt inspired by our power that toppled a decades-long authoritarian regime and sparked a wave of citizen action across the world. That's when I realised I come from a generation that started the first twenty-first century revolutions, a generation that changed the course of History, a bold generation that shaped its own destiny and that of future generations.

We have also challenged religious and historical constructs of male-only public spaces. In the Islamic tradition, the part of a funeral which takes place in the cemetery is reserved for men. However, the day the prominent politician Chokri Belaïd was buried after having been assassinated, women were present at the cemetery to pay our last respects.

During the revolution, I also learned to own my narrative. I started a Blog called Proudly Tunisian that was read by millions of people, where I reported, challenged mainstream narratives, and told the world that it was "our Revolution of Dignity not your Arab Spring." The Western media repeatedly wants to write and recreate our history in their own words, creating a false public memory. I blogged for hours, weeks, and months because I wanted to see our stories of agency and nonviolence become the mainstream news, not the exception. My blogs eventually made the headlines.

It started to stimulate debate and inform policy but also to bring more attention to issues of gender-based violence, rape, racism, and unequal inheritance.

Blogging was my catalyst of further political activism, a powerful tool to influence politics and amplify people's stories whose voices have been discounted in the formal process. Mainstream journalists and media organisations had long monopolised the reporting of local and international events. However, this time, the internet gave average citizens, especially young women, the ability to disrupt this control by using personal experiences to shape the narrative. Eventually, from just a platform for socializing, we turned social media into a tool for social change. Instead of being the subjects of news stories, we reported our own stories from the frontlines, live-tweeting the revolution, and in the process, with my compatriots, we forever changed the face of journalism and youth activism.

"I call for intergenerational co-leadership"
Africa Young Women Beijing+25 Manifesto

I did not see my father for six months until I joined him at the Choucha, a refugee camp at Ras Jdir that he had set up and had been managing on the Tunisian-Libyan borders following the fighting between pro-Gaddafi forces and rebels in Libya. About one million refugees, mostly African migrants, fled across the border into Tunisia. Understanding a parent's urge to ensure my security and protection, I had lied to him throughout the revolution and denied any involvement. I said I was studying, watching the news on TV, and staying at home. It was only after it was over that we had an intergenerational conversation.

"I was in the street," I said.

"I know," he nodded.

I did not expect that. I was waiting for his questions, ready to make my case, "Baba, I believe…"

He interrupted me before I finished. "You did it, your generation did the revolution," he said with warmth in his voice. "I respect that. I'm happy you're safe. Whatever you do next, I just want to know that you're safe."

It was such a relief to hear that. I ran into his arms, and we hugged in silence. He whispered in my ear, "You missed Angelina Jolie, though."

"Damn! Wasn't she tall, smart, fierce, and hot?" I said. "Lucky you." We both started laughing.

The Transition

The political landscape felt like we were holding the pendulum from one side with the dictatorship and when it fell, the pendulum swung in the extreme to the opposite side in one direction.

"But eventually it will be swinging back and forth in a slower motion until it finds its balance, so that's normal," I thought to myself.

The transition was not without its trauma. The activist I had become was quickly fed by violence. On the morning of April 9th, 2012, I was at Martyrs' Day. This public holiday commemorates the lives of people who died fighting for Tunisia's independence. During this protest, a huge body double my size, with a long sharp baton in hand, seized me by my hair, beat me, confiscated my camera, and insulted my mother.

I was arrested and taken to a police station full of angry men. It was terrifying and humiliating. I had to fight my phobia of policemen. I would walk across any policeman with a uniform, even a traffic police officer, and start shaking, my heart racing and my throat closing. The darkest truth about being a female is that it is always the people who are supposed to protect you who end up abusing you. I reminded myself when confronted with such adversity that if I fed my awareness with stillness and harnessed the power of my female intuition, I could always cultivate conscious reactions and decisions

Similarly, social media soon became a new battleground for both activists and the government. The authorities also created Facebook pages and started to mobilise online and created a lot of false information and harassment. Initially, it was difficult for the public to differentiate fact from fiction. More so, we found ourselves, young women, subjected to cyber assault. We became more vulnerable as our identities and opinions became public knowledge. My DMs were filled with insults and death threats.

Events started to unfold quickly, and everything escalated.

After a few visits to Cairo to support the movement that ousted another long-standing dictator, Hosni Mubarak, I was blacklisted from entering Egypt after being interrogated for twelve hours by the National Security Agency and then deported back to Tunis. I went to the Egyptian embassy to seek help and an explanation regarding my ban. Instead of helping me, the newly appointed ambassador harassed me.

'How come all this beauty is not allowed to enter Egypt?' he said in Egyptian dialect as he walked towards me.

I was speechless, and left immediately. I thought I could handle anything until a new situation came and I found myself powerless again. But this time I had had enough! I was not going to allow it. It was the first time I took action and reported harassment. I mobilised every decision maker I knew. Six months later, he was replaced.

I think I was rising from the ashes and out of powerlessness. It was a time of political consciousness for me.

I started to take more action not just to protest and "participate" but to actually create. I embraced the conviction that we should stop watching and blaming systems of oppression and actually take responsibility for our future.

A few weeks after Tunisia's revolution, a Senegalese Y'en A Marre—We have had enough—movement and Burkinabè Balai Citoyen—Citizen's Broom—movement started raising the same slogans. I put my skills to use for the next eight years of my journey. My vision for freedom took me to over thirty countries in Africa before I turned twenty-nine years old. I supported, trained, and worked with thousands of social movement leaders, feminist groups, artist collectives and youth activists across the continent on non-violence mobilisation, blogging, and organising, all of which I learnt by doing.

I've created multiple platforms for young people to speak up, be heard and take responsibility for their destiny; Voice of Women Initiative, Afrika Youth Movement, Afresist, Youth Programme of Holistic Empowerment Mentoring, Africa Inspire Kenya's conscious transformation, to mention a few.

Crossing colonial borders, living with people I had never met before, and experiencing Africanity made me feel at home in every corner of Africa. I started to see myself as a bridge across the Sahara; languages, cultures, stories, and beats. The Sahara where I come from that is meant to bridge us and not divide us has been labeling the northern part as Arab and closer to Europe and the Middle East, and the southern part as sub-Saharan and black. These overly simplistic and limiting colonial perceptions have been enforced across generations in our education and politics, fueling racism and Afrophobia.

Once conscious of this heritage, it was not enough to go around Africa as a young woman coming from the north of the Sahara trying to connect with the missing piece of her identity. I started to understand the history that connects us. I found the answer in Pan-Africanism. I was fascinated by the political solidarity during the independence movements in the face of colonial powers in the 60s which showed us how Pan-Africanism can liberate us.

Our African History taught me the essence of solidarity where young people at that time could organise with very little tools and no internet. Our African History also taught me that there is no Pan-Africanism without feminism. It is anti-Pan-African to reduce women to maternal functions or to seek to control their bodies, minds, and desires in the name of culture, faith, or any other excuse. It is anti-Pan-African to objectify women because objectification derives from colonialism and racism that was fought by Pan-Africanism. Therefore, patriarchy is a threat to Pan-Africanism.

The Africa We Want Is
"An integrated continent politically united and based
on the ideals of Pan-Africanism and the vision of
African Renaissance"
African Union Agenda 2063

It was such a revelation. My feminist activism has then become inseparable from my Pan-African identity.

When I found power in my voice as a Pan-African feminist, it became clear to me that the solution wasn't to fight back, but to create alternative spaces, non-violent and non-misogynistic spaces.

I stopped fighting to prove myself.

I started focusing on what I was good at—organising and galvanizing the collective power of young people.

We celebrated many victories supporting youth elected to office, preventing election violence, protecting human rights defenders, changing the narrative, and radicalizing more youth to our Pan-African movement instead of violent extremism.

The more I travelled, the more I realised that in our shared marginalisation, we could develop a sense of common identity and a critical consciousness that could enable us to challenge the status quo and lead.

Then, I was ready to lead.

I was prepared to serve. As former President of Malawi Joyce Banda said, "You must fall in love with the people that you serve, and they must also fall in love with you."

I was appointed as the first African Union Envoy on Youth and the youngest diplomat in the organisation with a mandate to advocate for the rights of about five hundred million young people in the fifty-five member states of the Union.

I worked to include young people across Africa in leadership positions rather than fighting our exclusion.

In South Sudan, I worked to promote young people as peacebuilders rather than gun-holders. As part of the campaign, I proudly witnessed over one thousand guns collected in voluntary disarmament.

By the time I finished my mandate, more young people were appointed to ministerial and other portfolios than ever since the 80s.

I started working for what was possible... rather than fighting what they told us wasn't.

I hadn't seen the difference before.

While navigating multilateral institutions, this leadership role did not protect me from experiencing ageism and sexism. I was fed, on a daily basis, portions of patriarchy, including chauvinism, mansplaining, and sexual harassment. It's still quite challenging as a woman to travel the continent, occupy leadership positions in male-dominated institutions, and work with a range of men. You still have to cross paths with those who don't take you seriously, and those who invite you "to finish the meeting in their hotel room."

There were a lot of meetings with Heads of States where the gatekeepers gave me the look of "What is this kid doing here?" I had to make allies, especially with senior women and elders in the intergovernmental space. These women opened the door for me.

There were instances when the UN Deputy Secretary-General Amina Mohammed would give me her seat in a manel panel (consisting entirely of men) at a closed diplomatic forum, or when Dr. Vera Songwe of the UN Economic Commission would have my back and put me on the front row of peace talk when they had thrown me at the back of the room to be invisible. I gained so much from women like them, even by just observing their leadership. I learnt that with every challenge there is an opportunity. I turned my frustration into innovation that often made the comfortable uncomfortable. Many were intimidated by my presence and resistant to change, but I eventually opened doors, spaces, and minds.

People tried so hard to stop me. I was criticised for even the shallowest things, such as the way I dressed to the office and to meetings. But why change who you are when others should get used to it, right? Instead of trying to restrict yourself to a space, make everyone get used to you. I gave it a week, two weeks, three months, six months... eventually people accepted my leadership style as a young female instead of contesting my leadership abilities. In fact, valuing femininity is an archetype for leadership.

There are more people who are not ready to accept women and youth in leadership roles than the contrary. But it all starts with believing in oneself, giving it your all, and working tirelessly. People did not get used to my presence, clothes, or age. I made those points irrelevant each time I spoke with intelligence, pertinence, and truth. I knew my facts. I was clear about the solutions. That's how I have claimed who I am in the spaces I move in, regardless of others' opinions. Eventually, people start to believe in what you do, most often when you leave that role. The legacy and impact on the institution unfolds regardless of one's age or gender.

"I champion partnerships for the goals"
United Nations Sustainable Development Goals

NalaFEM

I've been a noisy activist in anti-establishment spaces. Then I went into the belly of the beast. I understand both activism and policy making, and why there is a disconnect. I now feel more valuable to activists who want to influence policy. I envision Nala Feminist Collective (NalaFEM) as a bridge to fill the gap between policy and implementation, and between grassroots and intergovernmental spaces. I convened a council of seventeen women who have paved the way in different industries—from the first Black woman to win Miss Universe to the youngest minister in Africa. We have a platform, we have influence, we have a following—we have the power to really shake things up.

Our efforts are informed by our multi-layered sense of identity, mine as young, female, Tunisian, Mediterranean, Maghrebian with Amazigh indigenous roots, Arabic-speaking and living in post-colonial Africa. I have experienced harmful practices, gender-based violence, and dictatorship. Every council member of the Nala Feminist Collective also has a leadership journey, a story of a bold and daring super girl. All of us have managed to heal with kindness, compassion, honesty, and sisterhood. Female solidarity is possible and powerful. Knowing that you are not alone and coming together to reshape the future to be equal is powerful. It makes my liberation your liberation and my access your access in the face of patriarchy.

Our efforts are informed by our multi-layered sense of identity, mine as young, female, Tunisian, Mediterranean, Maghrebian with Amazigh indigenous roots, Arabic-speaking and living in post-colonial Africa. I have experienced harmful practices, gender-based violence, and dictatorship. Every council member of the Nala Feminist Collective also has a leadership journey, a story of a bold and daring super girl. All of us have managed to heal with kindness, compassion, honesty, and sisterhood. Female solidarity is possible and powerful. Knowing that you are not alone and coming together to reshape the future to be equal is powerful. It makes my liberation your liberation and my access your access in the face of patriarchy.

African women have been fighting for social change, equality, and democracy for more than a century. This decade, however, sees the emergence of a new generation of women. We, the millennials, use new means to fight for our rights and face our various struggles.

I am driven by the belief that our mark upon dignity and equality as African women will not go unrecognised and our experiences will not go unnoticed. NalaFEM is about putting my full truth out to the world and helping everyone else find their radical self. It is about supporting African women out there who are singing, racing, skating, dancing, and bossing; who own their lives and choose to wear makeup or be makeup free, to keep their natural hair or have no hair at all, to wear mini-skirts or wear the hijab, to have children or not, to get married or not. The important thing is that women choose.

That is what being a feminist leader means for me, an everyday activist. It means speaking up for myself and most importantly, changing the reality for other women, changing culture, and changing laws so that every woman can be free.

How can I not be a female leader? How can I not be a feminist when every day, every age, every experience is a reminder of my gender? Each step of my journey has prepared me for where I am and what I am able to build and nurture. My stories date far back to my childhood. I have vivid memories of it all. It's somehow healing to write it all in one place, instead of in notes and diaries here and there, but it's also painful. My eyes tear every time I think of it all—the journey. The times I was forced, the times I was humiliated, the times I allowed it. I still cry now but more out of pride than shame. Pride in how I love being a woman. I was made whole the moment I entered this world. I am a conscious objector to the status quo.

I am who I am because I'm the daughter of women warriors, thinkers, queens, and governors. They were Kahena the beret Zen Berber Queen of Aurès, Saïda Manoubia the saint, Aziza Othmana the princess of the Beylical dynasty, Tawhida Ben Cheikh the doctor, and Elissa the founder of Carthage to mention a few.

It is with the strength of these African female ancestors that in daily acts of choosing for myself, the woman in me turned Feminist.

The future of Africa is female, not because it's about the future, but because the past of Africa has also been female and it's a continuity of Africa.

Feminism has allowed me to strengthen my identity as Pan-African and made me realise clearly that it was not just about tasfih and family "honor." This is how patriarchy uses violence as a weapon to keep women trapped in inequality.

We must continue until this work is no longer necessary.

Conclusion

Last summer, I went to my cousin's engagement party. Everyone I greeted said "العاقبة لك"— "may you be next." Unfortunately, marriage and kids remain the ultimate success for a woman in our society. Everyone forgets the woman I am who hasn't taken a penny from her family since she graduated, who got herself a full scholarship on her own to finish her master's degree in the United Kingdom, and who forged her own path and became a young diplomat.

All of that doesn't matter. You are a woman and at the end of the day, and all you are recognised for is finding a man and raising kids, not because you choose to do so but because that is what is expected. After you hit your thirties, the pressure of what is expected only becomes stronger.

Again. Body. Battlefield. Others and their needs, wants and expectations. Sometimes I think, "I went through it all, I don't have to struggle anymore." But hélas! I still struggle every single day.

Every day is full of expectations of what a woman is and should be as a leader, a potential mother, a sister, a daughter ...

But in those moments, I hold my head high and say, "To hell with those expectations, to own me, my body, my choices, my life even, my vagina to give birth or not... I am going to be whatever the hell I want to be."

I carried many firsts in my family. I was the first to travel without a male guardian, the first to live abroad for work and school, the first in the family not to wear the Hijab... the only female to live in her own place independently, the first who doesn't treat marriage as an achievement and is still single at thirty-five years old (and rocking it may I add!)

Eventually, I cracked the glass ceilings to live differently from what culture and society expect, and even though my family and community still pressure me, they have stopped trying to force me to conform to social norms.

I continue to carry my childhood experiences and traumas, but I have turned them into resistance and a search for liberation. Fighting for liberation becomes a survival mechanism when patriarchy manifests in school, in gender roles, in public spaces, in transport, in the workplace. It becomes our daily resistance.

I know I will continue to drive change, whether from the street or the diplomatic rooms.

The place does not matter, what matters is to live one's mission.

We will be in those leadership positions sooner or later as those in power will not last forever so be well prepared. Small or big, make an impact in your community while being aware that we have the power and duty to positively change our societies.

Be coherent with yourself; coherence between what you believe, say, and do, is what makes you a true leader and changemaker.

Finding the radical in me and discovering every identity of mine has been a liberating experience. It has made me who I am today. That's why I believe it's crucial that you find yours, that it might bring you a step closer to knowing who you truly are and what you are capable of. Identity is not written on your passport or ID or whatever we are boxed into, be it race, religion, skin color, language, and what have you. In fact, finding your identity means unlearning all of that and learning who you really are.

Don't ignore it, deny it, or oppress it.

Instead, find it, recognise it, and liberate it.

Nourish it, cherish it, and celebrate it.

Breath it and act it.

Your power is your radical self.

CHAPTER TWO

Power with Purpose
by Ms. Bogolo Joy Kenewendo

"I am Nala because I challenge the status quo"

I, Bogolo Joy Kenewendo do solemnly swear that I will not directly or indirectly reveal the business of cabinet or proceedings or the nature of any documents or any other matter concerning the proceedings of cabinet except as maybe required by the discharge of the official duties or with the authority of the president.

A moment in history. A young African woman is appointed to a cabinet position, becoming the youngest female cabinet minister in Botswana's history and the youngest full cabinet minister in Africa. The moment is widely celebrated. Young people on the continent are hopeful that, they, too can rise to the highest of public offices and in this way help shape and define the world they live in. My appointment came as a surprise to most of the populace. To paraphrase Steve Jobs, the dots connect looking backwards. It was not luck that led me to this landmark moment. Rather, it was a culmination of dreams, beliefs, and hard work.

When I was young, my father used to ask me to make him tea in the early mornings after his cattle post visit or late in the afternoon after he had had his lunch. The tea was always accompanied by reading the newspaper or watching the news on television. I would sit beside him. This was crucial father-daughter time. This time spent bonding with my father opened me up to what was happening around the world. I became aware, from an early age, just how big the world was, and I took an active interest in the problems I read about or saw on TV.

I was disturbed by the war, famine, and political instability I saw raging around the world. What could a young girl in Motopi do about changing the world other than daydream about it while looking into the vast wilderness? My ambitions were not to be deterred by the vast wilderness I grew up in.

I wrote in a school essay that when I grew up, I wanted to be the United Nations Secretary General. Unfortunately, my sentiments were not met with celebration by those who deemed themselves more ambitious in their aspirations to become pilots or actors. All they heard was that I wanted to be a secretary.

In these precious moments spent with my father that got me termed "Daddy's girl," I learnt so much about the world. As a ten-year-old then, I learnt that we are all just a drop in the ocean, but even as a tiny drop, if we fall in the right places we can make rivers that flow into the oceans. Our impact can be immeasurable.

My father would take me to the cattle post and villages around ours in the Boteti region. We usually carried extra food and clothes to give to people we found wanting. In the face of poverty, I would be reminded that other people had it worse. In most families it would be said that "there are children starving in Africa." Though I never really liked that statement, it put things into perspective. Some of the families would barely have proper access to basic needs such as housing, running water, and food. Fortunately, my village still operated on a "take care of your neighbor" model and one would seldomly go to bed hungry. The need for care would become even clearer when children failed in their studies. Life options immediately became limited to a farm life dependent on remittances, if any. I started volunteering quite early on in life.

I didn't understand why some people needed so much. Why did I have clothes while others didn't? I started donating some of my clothes and my family's. I wanted to effect change. I wanted to have an impact. I yearned for a better world for all.

"I demand ending poverty"
United Nations Sustainable Development Goals

By the time I was sixteen, my volunteerism had gone from picking litter and donating clothes to being active at the Botswana National Youth Council. My time at the National Youth Council started what would be my journey in development practice. One day I saw a young man by the name Batsho Nthoi on the news talking about his role as Botswana's youth representative to the commonwealth and his work at the youth council. I was inspired, so much so that the next day my mother and I went to the youth center to find out how I could participate.

The youth center was the best incubator for leadership and development. It provided space for youth in the arts and a feeder program for politicians; many politicians got their start in politics and the policy space through the BNYC. This is where many youth issues were discussed. The youth council was a force to be reckoned with. It gave a voice to young people. It was through strong lobbying from the youth council that the Ministry of Youth was established, and the National Youth Policy subsequently adopted.

Being part of the youth center exposed me to the role of advocacy, the drafting of developmental policy, and the way government functions. By the time I was in my late teens, I wasn't only reading the news, I was also in the news with short articles on the inclusion of youth in decision making, representation in the United Nations, and some of the burning issues of the time.

My priorities were becoming clearer. Public policy was what I wanted to pursue and invest more time in. The youth council continued to provide me with opportunities to participate. I became Botswana's first youth representative at twenty-one years old to the United Nations General Assembly and Third Committee, a role I kept for two years. This role further expanded my world view of public policy, international relations, and development. I remember being at the United Nations and giving a speech alongside Secretary General Ban Ki Moon. Here I was, representing global youth in a speech to the Secretary General UNSG, calling for inclusive leadership, fast action on climate change, and the end of poverty.

> I was reminded of a question I once posed while trotting behind my father.
> "What traits does the UN SG possess?" I asked him.
> He said, "Integrity, compassion and most importantly, purpose."

It was during this time that my conversations with my father became more nuanced. My father was determined to make sure his daughter wasn't bogged down by talks of early marriage, children, or insinuations that I couldn't achieve anything I wanted. He would grunt disapprovingly whenever such topics were brought up or make statements to the effect of, "my daughter's future rests far beyond the kitchen. Who cares if she's not a good cook?" I'm a great cook now, but back then I couldn't even whip up a decent pot of pap. My best dish was a pan of fried eggs.

My conversations with my father reinforced my decision to go into public policy. When I graduated from university with a BA Economics, I knew I wanted to work in policy and grow as an aspiring economist. It was during this period that I was able to participate in youth advocacy as well as learn to be an economist.

As an economist, I dedicated a lot of time to learning more about making policy, providing advisory feedback on economic policy, and tracking trends that influence policy. I wrote a lot of working papers and participated in high level consultative meetings with Cabinet Ministers and Captains of industry.

All of the above moments led to my two oaths, one in parliament and one in cabinet. I remember sobbing during the national anthem, thinking of all the dreams and hopes past, present, and future. When the opportunity came, I served. I gave my all and I sacrificed. I believe the essence of who I am should always be reflected in my work. I have let those words guide me throughout my journey. In order to put these words into practice I believe leadership, and in particular servant leadership, are what tie them together and bring them to life.

I share this short story of a life lived thus far with purpose to remind you that it does not matter where you come from or what family you were born into; you can be whatever you want to be. My story started with humble beginnings, but it was these beginnings that provided purpose. You would think that as you rise this no longer matters, but trust me, this world still has many status quos that need to be challenged; gender, race, age, background, and family lineage, just to name a few.

I remember a very prominent member of society telling me I was a mistake in national leadership and that I should go back to the backwaters of wherever it is I had come from. People like me, what he called "nobodies," had no place at the table. This was obviously meant to hurt me, but I took it to mean I belonged on a bigger stage, at a more prominent table, on a larger platform. And so, I went out and claimed it! This is what you will face, as a young person, rising from "backwaters.".

Prepare yourself. Your validation doesn't come from outside; it should always come from within. Channel your roots, humility, and purpose. These will translate into how you choose to lead. Lead for people like yourself, for those who are told they don't belong, for those whose chances of making it to the table are miniscule. If you rise and make it through, make sure to make it count.

"Integrity, compassion, purpose." These words have echoed with me throughout my childhood into adulthood. My purpose has been closely aligned to inclusive leadership, economic agency, creating space for women and young people, and cultivating an economic revolution based on the legacies we have inherited. My purpose was always breathing down my neck with every turn I took; "mothanka ke ene yo." This loosely translates to "find a servant in me." I've heard this said so many times by the community leaders in my area. Nothing has resonated more with me. My journey is just getting started. I will keep serving!

Living The Legacy

Legacy refers to a bequest left behind for living and coming generations.

The generation that came before us stood up and said *no* to colonialism. They sought and fought for independence. This generation stood on the principle of "African decisions about Africa are to be made in Africa." These political and revolutionary leaders who brought Africa its first wave of independence were young. Patrice Lumumba led a revolution at age twenty-nine. He became the first Prime Minister of the Republic of Congo at the age of thirty-four and was assassinated the following year, at age thirty-five.

Graça Machel was thirty years old when she became the Minister of Education in Mozambique. Kwame Nkrumah, Sir Seretse Khama, and Julius Nyerere were in their late thirties and early forties.

What, then, is the African spirit? Is it country specific? For example, what is the Botswana spirit? What made people in their thirties rally for change and not starve to death?

We recall that earlier generations fought fascism and communism not just with missiles and tanks, but with sturdy alliances and enduring convictions. They understood that our power alone cannot protect us, nor does it entitle us to do as we please. Instead, they knew that our power grows through its prudent use. Our security emanates from the justness of our cause, the force of our example, and the tempering qualities of humility and restraint.

I often wonder if there is an African spirit that we should enforce, encourage, and develop in order to ensure that we rally together for the betterment of this country and the continent as a whole. I'm sure in poor Botswana in the 1970 and 80s, the thought of building a fully-fledged university such as the University of Botswana seemed like a huge challenge, and for us today it may feel daunting to build our economy. An economy that is transformational, that provides opportunities to better our lives, and that is people centered. An economy that is not only responsive to today's challenges but also primes us for tomorrow's opportunities.

What is the clarion call that we need to make? We need growth, we need transformation, and we need jobs, and we need them now. We can't wait for long. We have been waiting for too long. Sometimes, the only reasonable thing to do is to be unreasonable. This is how innovation and reinvention happen.

Let us further recognise that the challenges we face moving forward will require combined efforts and collective sacrifice. We should be mindful of the fact that, regardless of the development strides we have made, we are still very much a developing society located within a still marginalised continent.

If we are to attain the levels of development that we aspire to, we also need to resuscitate our Pan-African principles of self-reliance and unity, for, to quote Kwame Nkrumah, "we share not merely a common history, but a common destiny."

The Africa We Want Is
"An Africa as a strong, united, resilient and
influential global player and partner"
African Union Agenda 2063

Inclusive and Diverse Leadership for Impact

In the recent past we have had women contribute significantly to our development and success. There is Mabel Dove Danquah, who is a journalist, political activist, FEMINIST, and the first African woman to be elected by popular vote to parliament in 1954. There is Asmaa Mahfouz, a modern-day revolutionary who is credited with sparking the January 2011 uprising in Egypt through a video blog post encouraging others to join her in protest in Tahrir Square. She is considered one of the leaders of the Egyptian Revolution and is a prominent member of Egypt's Coalition of the Youth of the Revolution.

Many argue that Gender shouldn't be a factor in whether or not a person can be a great leader--a person's leadership abilities should depend on their individual strengths and personality traits. However, we know it does.

Women are inclined towards a holistic and self-reflective approach. They are leaders who share their knowledge and are able to connect with their colleagues so as to help the team and the business. When women bring this attitude into managerial roles, it may actually make them stronger and more-effective leaders.

Greater involvement of women results in a broader perspective on the crisis at hand. It paves the way for the deployment of richer and more complete solutions than if they had been imagined by a homogeneous group.

Women are better at managing the crisis better than their male counterparts. Resilience, pragmatism, benevolence, trust in collective common sense, mutual aid, and humility are mentioned as common features of the success of these women leaders.

According to existing research on gender and leadership, leadership styles can be categorised either as masculine or feminine. Masculinity and agenticism relate to traits associated with male leadership, such as being assertive, controlling, aggressive, ambitious, dominant, forceful, independent, self-confident, and competitive. Agentic characteristics are ascribed more strongly to men than women. On the other hand, feminine or communal characteristics are ascribed more strongly to women than men and describe primarily a concern of the leader with the welfare of other people. For example, women are associated with being affectionate, helpful, kind, sympathetic, interpersonally sensitive, nurturing, and gentle.

We observe that in these ecosystems, leadership is driven by supposed "feminine qualities"—empathy, compassion, listening, and collaboration.

These are distinct from the characteristics associated with the exercise of traditional managerial, supervisory, and controlling power. We are seeing a societal shift toward feminine leadership and women have an upper hand here.

Women are perceived by their managers—particularly their male managers—to be slightly more effective than men at every hierarchical level and in virtually every functional area of the organisation. It is still unfortunate that only three of SADC countries have over 30% of women in economic decision making. Why is this so?

Leaders need to take a hard look at what gets in the way of promoting women in their organisations. Clearly, the unconscious bias that women don't belong in senior level positions plays a big role. It's imperative that organisations change the way they make hiring and promotion decisions and ensure that eligible women are given serious consideration.

That said, for centuries there have been broad cultural biases against women and stereotypes die slowly. We therefore need to be proactive in getting more women in leadership. First, we create an enabling environment by how we lead.

1. Start them young. Offer mentorship to young girls.

2. Offer career guidance based on a future that is skills-based. If we get young women to pursue skills-based careers, we will not have an excuse later of a shortage of women in certain professional fields.

3. Create succession. Introduce graduate programs that can identify those with potential and mentor them.

4. Walk the talk: what we talk about in seminars of empowerment should turn to practice. Ensure policies are inclusive and recognise women's abilities.

5. Offer packages that are deliverables-focused instead of time-focused and that pay well. Incentivise women.

6. Deal with unconscious bias. Ask, "are we succumbing to unconscious bias? Are we automatically giving the nod to a man when there's an equally competent woman?"

7. Are you a multiplier or a diminisher?

8. Have more inclusive conversations. Bring males into conversations about gender. They should be part of the plenary conversation.

9. Beware of female antagonism between women. Coming from a place of limited positions, we must banish the mindset that we can only have one woman at the top. Banish tokenism. Build and empower accountability that checks the progress you have made.

Our fight for Women leadership is based on consequential leadership. We need women leaders who want to make a world-changing difference. We need women leaders with impact.

"I call for economic justice"
Africa Young Women Beijing+25 Manifesto

Q&A with The Author

1. What was your first dream?

My first dream was to be a leader. It was to help people. Coming from one of the poorest regions in Botswana, I believed we could be better. I wanted to get involved in policy making and change life for the better for many of the poor I saw growing up. My career path as an Economist and politician were inspired by His Excellency former President Festus Mogae who led the transformation of Botswana from a poor to a middle-income country. As a mentor, he made me believe that these career paths could create change and directly impact the lives of many.

2. What does Confidence mean to you?

It means trusting yourself, your abilities, and your voice.

3. What does Opportunity mean to you?

Space needs to be claimed, not assumed. Opportunity comes in different forms, some obvious and some not so obvious. However, not all opportunities are ideal for you. Learn discernment and pick opportunities that align with your vision and your purpose for your life.

4. How do you start your day to achieve the objectives you have set for yourself?

I work out, meditate, plan my day over a cup of coffee and check off my to do list at lunch and end of day. I end the day by reading at least five pages of a book or an article.

5. How important is discipline when it comes to building a fulfilling career?

It is everything. No dream can be pursued and realised without discipline.

6. What has been the most important skill that you've developed in your professional journey?

The first skill is leadership This second skill is the ability to constantly learn and grow my knowledge base. This makes me adaptable to different situations and posts. This has led to cultivating servant leadership. It's very important to keep a large team motivated and to make sure the public are part of the development process.

7. What is the value of a role model?

Role models provide inspiration. They help you envision what is attainable in life and motivate you to raise the bar of what is deemed achievable. However, it's important to know that we are all human and recognise and accept the flaws inherent in all of us, especially our role models. No one should be placed on a pedestal.

8. What would be your advice to young women overcoming social and economic adversity?

You can overcome. Your background doesn't define you. Believe in yourself and where you are going and surround yourself with mentors who can help you in your journey. FOCUS!

9. How do you manage disrupters/toxicity to your journey?

I remind myself why I started the work I do in the first place. Also, meditation helps.

10. How do you turn fear and failure into strength and opportunity?

I allow myself to feel the fear and work through it. I remind myself that adrenaline is life fuel for strength when channeled properly. Failure is mere redirection, and, to quote the cliché, "when one door closes another opens." But you have to do something about it.

11. What is the best career advice you were given?

Try to find humor in the difficult situations. It will keep you sane.

12. What is your daily motto?

If you can dream it, believe it. Make it happen.

13. Name a book that inspired you.

I have two; one I read when I was about fourteen or fifteen, *The Tipping Point* by Malcom Gladwell, and the other one, *The Originals* by Adam Grant, when I was around twenty-eight. I think I read them more than a decade apart. They both reinforced the need to embrace one's originality and the belief that one can make a difference.

14. What would your younger self tell you if she were to meet you now?

You are enough! Focus on what you want and be wary of opportunities that aren't meant for you. When you find yourself tempted by what's not yours, ask yourself, does this help me with my purpose? Don't forget to enjoy the ride. Live a little!

15. How would you advise the new generation of activists advocating for gender equality and women empowerment?

Things are bound to get harder before they get better. Don't despair. The baton has been handed over to us. We must start the change from where we stand by creating inclusive spaces and bringing more allies along with us. Let's be bolder and demand the change we deserve. It is our birth right!

CHAPTER THREE

Adansonia Digitata
by Ms. Martine Kessy Ekomo Soignet

"I am Nala
because together we are powerful
drivers of change"

My first memories go back to when I was three years old. I remember myself as a little girl full of life. I was a very curious child. I carried an unconditional love for my mother, Lina, my sister Ingrid, and my big brothers, Tanguy and Brice.

Tanguy is three years older than me. I was fascinated by the games he invented with his friends. At age three, I didn't understand why I was told that these were games meant only for boys. My mother still recounts the multiple times I came back to her crying because an aunt would not let me play with my brother. I began to wonder how running, climbing, jumping in puddles, laughing until one rolled on the ground, dancing in the rain, and imitating our superheroes on television were "boys' games." At age three, I had already begun sensing prejudice and injustice, which could be quite rare for a child. I felt deprived of a freedom that was rightfully mine. Now, I can now shout it out loud: I viscerally envied my older brother's freedom, his "right to play."

My aunts always implored me to be "wise." My hair was often styled in pigtails and decorated with colored pearl elastics. I still have plenty of pictures from this period. When I look at them, I think I looked cute and pretty. However, I did not understand the link between being pretty and the obligation not to play "boys' games."

I yearned to explore my imagination and fully experience my adventurous character while playing my brother's games. It was during our games that I felt most free. Meanwhile, I was pressured by my aunts and other family members to abandon this "unacceptable behavior." I began playing less and less with Tanguy and created a world for myself in which I sailed—alone. I didn't have many friends, or at least their company tired me quickly. I turned to writing and drawing.

I started to pay more attention to what my mother was doing.

My mother, Mrs. Lina Ekomo-Ikoli, is a character from a novel.

She comes from a wealthy family but has not only known beautiful days. She was forced to make choices she still assumes to this very day, such as living with a man (my father) who was just a flirt after her mother-in-law asked her father to kick her out of the house. She carried this feeling of familial betrayal throughout her life. It made her stricter with herself and especially combative to prove to her father that she was not what her mother-in-law said about her. She was an educated woman who chose to continue her studies and pursued a master's in Sociology while pregnant with my little brother Daniel, the sixth of the siblings. At the time, she was also working as a Communication Specialist for the United Nation Development Program (UNDP). She showed me that a woman can do everything and pursue her dreams.

During the war in the 90s, my mother had to deal with my father's shortcomings. I have memories of a woman who took care of everything, all the time. She paid for the education of her eight children, did all the grocery shopping at home, made sure we had toys, had kind words for us every day and hugged us in our moments of distress. She stood fierce, with a rare elegance and a temperament that was a mix of both fire and softness.

Her favorite perfume, which she has worn ever since I was a child, is "J'adore" from Dior. It is one of the most powerful perfumes that my senses have immortalised. When I think of her, melon and jasmine flood my mind.

I have seen my mother cry alone, mainly because of my father's behavior, or at other times because she struggled to make ends meet and couldn't pay for our education. What impressed me was her ability to bounce back from her sadness. She always took care of us. In my imagination, my mother was acting. I couldn't fathom how one's body and soul could suffer from immense sorrow and still be able to get up the next day and do the work that needed to be done.

I loved visiting her at work every day after my classes ended. I would sit and observe her behind her gigantesque desktop computer with her glasses and a stack of files on her table. At work, she became a different person. She exuded more confidence. Even the tone of her voice was different from the tone she used at home. I would imitate her by putting my little feet in her shoes and her lipstick on my lips and stand in front of the mirror in her room.

The Descent

In 1996, I turned six years old. It was my first experience of war. The war started when the Central African Army did not receive their salaries, which the State hadn't paid out in three years, and mutinied against President Ange Félix Patassé. We lived in the city center of Bangui, the capital of the Central African Republic.

I didn't understand what was happening around me. One morning, we heard gunshots coming from somewhere in the city. My mother ordered us to stay inside the house. We hid behind the strongest wall. Days and weeks passed. We remained locked in our family house. Our food changed—from diverse and colored foods, such as cassava leaves or chicken and sauce, to meager rations of rice porridge. Our parents no longer laughed.

My mother wore a serious face. There were often great moments of silence, when only the national radio and RFI (Radio France Internationale) could be heard in the house. We listened anxiously to statements from the army that had mutinied and tried to keep abreast of the war.

Gradually, members of our extended family came to take refuge with us. In these moments of sadness, the arrival of my cousins brought life back to the house. We allowed ourselves to play and escape the gravity of the adult world, the war, and what we only half understood.

The Journey

One morning, we heard a loud, frightening boom near our house. It was the sound of bombs. Mother said we had to leave. She packed our bags in silence, stuffing things inside our suitcases in rapid, nervous movements. I carried a few toys and my favorite Bart Simpson shorts in my little panda-shaped backpack.

We understood that we were living in an important moment.

We were put in a rickshaw with our luggage. My uncle came along as our security guard. We rode in the rickshaw for a short while, and then we were told to get out. It could take us no farther. The nearest town, Bimbo, was nine kilometers away. We began our long walk, crossing abandoned neighborhoods. We crouched behind car tires to hide from the patrols of soldiers on the prowl. We even hid underground, in the sewers. Finally, we arrived at my uncle Pastor Charles's home.

We learned that after we had left our family home, a shell crashed into one of the rooms—the very room our parents had asked us to take refuge in at the height of the fighting. My uncle Simeon received shrapnel in his arm. Our dog, Grace, was killed instantly.

We lived with my uncle for several weeks. I don't really remember how long exactly. During this period, we witnessed many funerals, tears, cries, and prayers for peace in the neighborhood we lived in. This moment gave me life's first lesson: it is possible to lose everything overnight. I was only six years old. There was so much going on inside me, and though I did not understand everything, I paid attention to what was going on around me. This experience of the war had a profound effect on me.

"I call for silencing the guns"
Africa Young Women Beijing+25 Manifesto

I began to think about what and who I wanted to be. The answer I gave myself was clear: I would become a children's lawyer and help children who had lost one or both parents, who were being physically or verbally abused, or who had also experienced the violence and trauma I saw around me.

At the age of nine, I became more certain I wanted to become a children's lawyer. It was as though my whole being was preparing to become this dreamed future self. I began to mimic trial scenes in front of the mirror. I used tablecloths to make lawyer's dresses. At that time, I didn't have access to the Internet. I watched a lot of television. I became a fan of detective series such as the French TV show Julie Lescot, in which lawyers defend their clients. There is magic when training in front of a mirror. I married my dream, I nourished my indignation, I watered my ambitions and gradually, I was able to put into words what I was feeling inside.

I thought about the impact I wanted to make as a lawyer. Becoming a lawyer would not be enough. I had to become the kind of lawyer who carried the voice of the voiceless.

NalaFem

I can trace the ease with which I express myself in front of an audience, whoever that audience is, to those childhood years spent rehearsing in front of the mirror.

When I was seven, our parents decided to send us abroad. The first time was to the Ivory Coast, where I went with all my brothers and sisters, and the second time was to a boarding school in Benin together with my brothers and sisters again. When I returned to Bangui, my parents decided it was time to send me to France to continue my studies—alone. At ten, this was heartbreaking. Once again, due to the war, I found myself leaving my parents. For the first time, I had to learn how to live without my brothers and sister. I didn't know that the distance between us would last for the next fifteen years.

I was sent to live with my aunt in the suburbs of Paris, in Saint-Denis in the 93rd department. It was not the type of environment I knew or was accustomed to.

On my first day of school, I heard one of my classmates say to another, "Nique ta mère!"

The other one answered, "Ta mère la grosse pute!"

I burst into tears. These swear words shocked me. The CPE was forced to send me home because I could not stop crying. I called my mother and begged her to send me back home despite the instability of the country. She refused. That felt like a slap— a betrayal.

I spent a little more than fifteen years in France, including five years in the suburbs of Paris. These were crucial, formative years. They shaped my career, especially my commitment to the feminist struggle.

While at home there were ups and downs related to my conflicted relations with some of my cousins, my daily life with my classmates pushed me to revolt. I realised that they were on another planet most of the time, especially when I compared their attitudes and ways of living to the realities of my country.

They had the chance to go to school, but they preferred to skip. They spent their time stealing, lying, and disrespecting adults. The worst part was when they attacked me, calling me a "bledarde" and a "buffoon" because I spoke perfect French, without slang, and was one of the best students in class.

My dream of becoming a lawyer remained close to my heart. However, I missed my country and my parents. When my aunt installed a desktop computer with AOL connection packages, I spent more time learning about the origin and the history of the conflicts in the Central African Republic than trying to understand law. The more I read, the more I became indignant. I scribbled down ideas for solutions. Yes, at the age of twelve or thirteen, I had already begun to make my contribution to the resolution of my country's crises. I saw myself playing a key role. My suburban classmates taught me plenty. By observing their behavior, I understood that they were young like me— that a nation is built on its youth. And that it was as important to protect and accompany them from an early age.

It followed naturally that I studied social, economic, and political sciences. This is how I entered the world of geopolitics.

Finally, after fifteen years abroad, I decided to return to my country and contribute to its recovery. I have often been asked why I decided to leave a stable and fulfilled life in France to return to my country at the end of 2013.

It was one of the tensest moments of the inter-community crisis. To be honest, each time I try to respond to that question, I simply forget how to arrange my words or my ideas so as to birth coherent answer. My decision to return and work for peace was "visceral."

Have you ever experienced the "obvious"? Like what you feel when you fall in love and your heart understands it but your brain tries to rationalise it? I was madly in love with my country, without really knowing why. I knew I had to go back even if it meant disobeying and hurting my parents. I cried a lot before leaving France. There were times when I considered myself crazy for making this decision.

The crisis in which I live today in the Central African Republic and the work I have been doing with young people since my return has given meaning to my life, to my choices, and to my history. I am the first geopolitical analyst of the Central African Republic. The issues of peace and security on the continent have a different echo when I work with young people. Such positioning allows me to distance myself from those meetings within national and especially international institutions in which words fuse but only have inaction as an echo. Daily, the young people in my country go beyond theories by taking actions that put individuals back at the center of their communities, more specifically young women.

"I champion peace, justice and strong institutions"
United Nations Sustainable Development Goals

The founding father of my country, Barthelemy Boganda, spoke of the "Zo Kwe ZO," which in French translates to "Chaque personne est une personne" --each person is a person, full of life, fears, hopes, ideas, projects, and talents.

It took on even more meaning for me when, in the evolution of my career, I saw how young women were being erased, and moreover, how they are forced to remain "victims" of the ongoing crisis. They are not recognised for their tremendous contributions to peace building.

I emphasise that the young people of the Central African Republic are not figures on a report, but people who, despite a hostile environment, remain committed to the peace and development in our country.

I have had to intervene in several forums at the national and international level and I have always had this feeling—that the voice of young women still carries the "syndrome of the cute" that I encountered as a child: our presence is applauded, beautiful photos are taken, but the effective consideration of our projects and our ideas are not valued. This is a reality for youth in general. It is much worse for young women.

This marginalisation and this "cute" syndrome are coupled with a "glass ceiling" that is unfortunately held by many of the women leaders we rely on. The "glass ceiling" I am talking about here refers to the feeling that as a young woman, my ambitions represent a threat to women in the older generation who fought for access to the spaces they move in today. They do not fail to remind us of this on every occasion.

I refuse to believe that being a geopolitical analyst is a "boys' game." I don't feel "cute" or "special" or "favored" when I speak before leaders or the UN Security Council. I feel committed and concrete in my ideas. I feel determined and responsible. I believe this feeling is shared by many other committed young women when they stand before decision-making bodies.

This pushes me to talk about the new generations of young women who want to engage in the field of research and peace building. I assume my desire to become a model because I remain convinced that the more women in these fields and arenas, the more consistent, practical, and concrete the efforts for peace will be.

Becoming a role model for many young people (girls or boys) is like a religious commitment: it requires rigor at all levels, both in one's private and public life. It is necessary to lead by example. That is what I have tried to do throughout my journey. This vocation also comes with moments of doubt and frustration that usually develop when we have the feeling that people do not understand what we are trying to do, or the ideas were are trying to transmit. These moments taught me to question myself in constructive ways without rejecting even the most critical comments I received.

This reminds me of a very difficult time.

At the time, President Faustin Archange Touadéra had decided to appeal to Russia, through the Wagner Group, to fight the rebellion that had plagued the country for years. This decision led to a wave of anti-Western sentiments in the population, particularly from the diaspora, which is very present on social networks. I was invited by the United Nations Security Council to intervene as an activist in the situation in the Central African Republic. After my speech was broadcast online, a wave of hatred poured forth on my person on social networks. Indeed, I had to endure online assaults launched by an online user who claimed to be a Pan-Africanist and therefore against Western presence and "their manipulations" on the continent while the latter lived in France. This online user was followed immensely by an audience of African and Central African diaspora.

This pushes me to talk about the new generations of young women who want to engage in the field of research and peace building. I assume my desire to become a model because I remain convinced that the more women in these fields and arenas, the more consistent, practical, and concrete the efforts for peace will be.

Becoming a role model for many young people (girls or boys) is like a religious commitment: it requires rigor at all levels, both in one's private and public life. It is necessary to lead by example. That is what I have tried to do throughout my journey. This vocation also comes with moments of doubt and frustration that usually develop when we have the feeling that people do not understand what we are trying to do, or the ideas were are trying to transmit. These moments taught me to question myself in constructive ways without rejecting even the most critical comments I received.

This reminds me of a very difficult time.

At the time, President Faustin Archange Touadéra had decided to appeal to Russia, through the Wagner Group, to fight the rebellion that had plagued the country for years. This decision led to a wave of anti-Western sentiments in the population, particularly from the diaspora, which is very present on social networks. I was invited by the United Nations Security Council to intervene as an activist in the situation in the Central African Republic. After my speech was broadcast online, a wave of hatred poured forth on my person on social networks. Indeed, I had to endure online assaults launched by an online user who claimed to be a Pan-Africanist and therefore against Western presence and "their manipulations" on the continent while the latter lived in France. This online user was followed immensely by an audience of African and Central African diaspora.

In targeting me, he spread false information and led an aggressive onslaught against my person and even went so far as to question my identity. For many, my name did not "sound Central African enough." Others said, "She does not speak French like a Central African," or, "She has a Cameroonian face," or, "She is a lesbian, just see her hair." (I wear frizzy hair in dreadlocks.) And so on and so forth. Other online live users, this time from the Central African Republic, went so far as to attack my family. My sin, according to them, was to have "usurped" the place of the Minister of Foreign Affairs and thus to be an instrument of "Westerners."

I did not understand how my own fellow citizens could reject me in the name of a theory created from scratch by a stranger I had never heard of.

This has been one of the most difficult moments in my journey thus far. Thanks to the support of my family, colleagues, and friends, I managed to get through this trying time and regain my self-confidence—this time with more rage and determination. I let my creativity explode through art with the artist name, "WALI," which means "Woman" in our national language, Sango. I also expressed my creativity through my research, analysis, and incubation of sustainable social and economic projects in the Central African Republic. This project is called Peace & Development Watch--Central African Republic. I also opened my "GE" themed store, which means 'here' in our national language, and which celebrates the beauty of the Central African Republic and promotes talents and local artists. A first for the country.

I have come to understand that committing to peace goes beyond theories and a mere targeting of actors (in my case, youth). It relies on creating a positive and inspiring dynamic. For me, peace is made up of multiple layers of positive and unifying actions, in this way working towards a vision that centers well-being and the common good. Moreover, it promotes a world that embraces the diverse peoples who form a nation. I embraced once again the vision of our founding father Barthelemy Boganda which is that of the "ZO KWE ZO" —a vision of the Central African dream that joins that of many African countries.

My life in the Central African Republic has also taught that war is not eternal. It is necessary to think about the future with strength and courage. We need to fight against the socio-cultural constraints that undermine the effective participation of youth and women in public life and in their communities.

It requires a lot of selflessness, conviction, and action. We must be the active voices and the hands of the peace that we all call for. How? By going beyond our theories and being concrete. My eyes are fixed on this daily vision.

It is akin to planting a seed of hope, like that of the Adansonia Digitata, commonly known in our communities as the Baobab. This slow-growing tree has an exceptionally long lifespan. It is common to encounter specimens that arc nearly two thousand years old. Thus, it is about accepting that change does not happen overnight. We need to be patient, and above all we must continue to create spaces where we celebrate our unity, our diversity, and our humanity.

I don't think I'll live long enough to fully enjoy the fruits of this work. I like to think I'm one of those who are contributing to our collective future by forging a solid foundation for future generations. One day, the torch will pass from our competent and vigilant hands to theirs.

Similar to the African Baobab, the most useful tree in the Sahel, these young women and men will produce new generations united by strong common values that will make our continent a peaceful, inclusive, and indivisible land.

The Africa We Want Is
"A peaceful and secure Africa"
African Union Agenda 2063

CHAPTER FOUR

Activism Starts with One Story

by Ms. Oluwaseun Ayodeji Osowobi

"I am Nala because I believe in service and community action"

Growing Up as a Young Girl in Nigeria

I am from a considerably well to do family. I attended one of the most expensive and quality secondary schools in my locality. While some children attended government schools, only a few attended private schools. Others joined neighbourhood "lessons" (a word used for educational classes that are taken outside the setting of a registered school). Others didn't get any form of education. Outside school, girls, myself included, were domesticated from a young age while the boys played football or rolled tyres out in the dust or outside. Though I was privileged, it did not shield me from the social and cultural vices girls face, such as physical child abuse (beating) from neighbours and witnessing domestic violence within my neighbourhood and extended family.

My experiences as a teenager solidified the activist I am today. I noticed that while boys had the leverage to play with their peers after completing their school assignments or right after school, girls were expected to stay indoors and do chores. Why couldn't I hang out with my friends like the boys did? I was told by family, relatives, and church members that I needed to shield my innocence from boys' "wild thoughts and behaviours." This didn't make sense to me. Why should my existence be tied to a cultural notion of purity that belied the fact that in the real world, I would still need to interact with these same boys I was advised to avoid?

Not only did I experience girls' social segregation from boys, I also saw how girls and women were ill-treated by society. Though I seldom saw intimate partner violence first-hand, the culture of spousal violence, in which women were beaten by their husbands, was a known and accepted phenomenon in my community. When these women tried to leave their marriages, their families would force them to return "home."

In what world is it permissible that the victim of the crime be forced to return to the crime scene? I was troubled by the violence these women experienced. I became sensitive to how women's bodies are regarded as a holding place for men's destructive and aggressive impulses.

In most rural and semi-rural areas, there was and still is an unwritten rule that the way to measure a woman's strength and value is in how domesticated she is. Women will pursue economic opportunities during the day such as office work or trading at the market, and then return home to labour in the kitchen. In my locality, I often saw women who, tired and exhausted from work, cooked late into the evening, but I never saw men do the same. This built resistance in me. Men were fond of watching football and reading the newspaper, while the women did all the house chores.

I felt rage at this injustice. Why did men have it better than women? In some cases, the women in my neighbourhood would juggle cooking, cleaning, tending to the children, and helping them with their school assignments, all at the same time. I know African women are heroes, but *heroes sef dey rest*—heroes also deserve to rest. In many households today, women and men contribute equally to the family's financial needs. Hence, why do most men contribute next to nothing domestically?

**"I am Nala
because I believe in service and
community action"**

My father worked up North, so I shuttled between Lagos and his location throughout my teens and into my adulthood. Moving from the southern part of Nigeria to the North, I had a seemingly similar yet different experience. I saw another prevalent form of violation: child marriage. In my neighbourhood and at the local market, I saw young girls with babies strapped to their backs. Who were the fathers? How can we consider that a child is old enough to conceive but ineligible to vote, drive, or make decisions? Not long after, I heard of a young girl in a neighbourhood who was being prepared for marriage to a man older than her father.

I had no power to change it or make a difference; such matters were discussed by "the elders," who are mostly men. It is standard practice that young girls in the North are groomed and prepared for marriage from the age of eleven, while their counterparts in the South are in school. For some, it's based on religious beliefs, while for others, it's a debt repayment process. A father who owes a wealthy man money or land could marry off his daughter to pay off his debt.

Sadly, nothing much has changed in the last twenty years. Such religious and social norms still hold prominence in our day to day lives and practices. Child marriage, which is a form of child abuse, remains prevalent in Nigeria and continues to have grave effects. A recent report during the pandemic found that married girls are denied their fundamental rights to education, safe dwelling, and freedom from violence, and often do not have adequate health care.

Without strong regulatory protections for girls, families continue to force them into early marriage, citing religious and traditional practices as well as a desire to avoid the social stigma caused by teen pregnancy (Human Rights Watch, 2022).[1]

My Reality: Violence Related to Elections

The turning point for me came in 2011 when I was drafted into the National Youth Service Corps (NYSC). I was excited to travel to a different state to serve my nation. Similar to military training, anyone who passes through this phase is considered to have undergone paramilitary training and is called a "corper." I was posted to my place of primary assignment (PPA) to teach English at a secondary school in a remote location.

The next phase was the General election process. Corpers are posted outside the PPA to ensure a free and fair election process where no one is influenced or coerced to make decisions. I was posted to a village where a prominent community member was vying for office. I was the only female corper posted there. It was like being thrown into the lion's den.

My polling unit was quiet. Nothing much happened until I was approached to register underage children so as to make them eligible to vote. The trouble ahead was more damning. The prominent community member who was vying for office offered me an enticing job opportunity. I rejected the offer and was punished heavily for it. The community members became hostile towards me for refusing to register underage children and help boost the number of registered voters for their candidate the son of the soil's victory. In the face of this hostility, the first friendly person who approached me seemed safe.

1. Human Rights Watch (2022) Nigeria: Child Marriage Violates Girls' Rights, pp. 2.

NalaFem

It seemed like an excellent strategy to have someone on my side. I was raped by this person who posed as a friend.

This was a difficult time in my life. I thought upholding my values should keep me safe. I thought demanding a better system and getting qualified leaders into political seats was an excellent service to our nation. Was I foolish to think this way? Was it a selfless service or an act of pride to show I had standards? A lot went through my mind. I felt anger and pain. I felt dirty. I questioned my moral justifications and religious beliefs. I cried for days and could not process my emotions. I felt filthy and did not know how to deal with what had happened. There were no formal or available structures to assist me and respond to what I had gone through.

It was at this moment that my purpose came to me. There was an awakening in my spirit to do something. How many more women and girls like myself had to suffer before something was done? I felt rage and decided to channel it to create change. I decided to brush up on my knowledge of issues around gender equity and violence against women and girls. I applied for a master's degree program in International Relations with a focus on human rights and gender at Swansea University and moved to the United Kingdom in 2011 to start a new phase of my life. Honestly, this was also a getaway moment from Nigeria to reflect on my life and self-heal. It's okay to leave places where the abuse occurred so you can breathe and catch your breath.

I understood, on a deeper level, the dangers of violence against women and girls and the impact on their physical well-being, mental health, and stability. Though my experience differs from what other women may have faced, oppression and injustice are cut from the same socio-cultural fabric.

NalaFem

Following My Passion: Building STER (Stand to End Rape Initiative)

It is 2013. I begin to read stories on social media and Nigerian dailies about rape, with the victims' personal information boldly shared while the identities of the alleged perpetrators are shielded. In addition, the stories barely provide information about available resources the survivors can access. Neither do they aim to enlighten or condemn the rape crimes or take any other measures to prevent their recurrence. A light bulb turns on in my head. I decide to move back to Nigeria.

It felt like a voice was speaking to me to move back and help fix the problems I'd identified. It was a heavy burden on my spirit but also a crazy adventure. I reconnected with a secondary schoolmate who was volunteering at the United Nations Headquarters in New York. They informed me of an internship vacancy they had seen posted on Facebook. I applied and got an unpaid internship as a Communications and Administrative Intern at the United Nations Headquarters in New York. It was an exciting opportunity. I was the youngest applicant at the time, and it was the first time a master's student from my university was offered the position.

I was excited by the prospect of building a different life for myself. I had a secondary school classmate at the UN and we both had the dream of making a name for ourselves there. I set out to the UN with hope and a desire to make a change. I enjoyed working at the organisation and living in New York, save for the daily work routine, the dirty air, and the exhausting commute to work.

I felt burdened in my spirit and inspired to follow my passion and make a tangible impact in the lives of everyday Nigerians. I knew I needed to gain useful insight and knowledge on the issue of gender and human rights.

I worked at the UN for three months and then moved to another organisation, Half the Sky Movement (now known as Show of Force) to focus on research in social and behavioural change. This allowed me to specifically learn new programming strategies and gain insights into storytelling. Through my work at Half the Sky Movement, I tackled many social issues affecting women and girls, such as sexual violence, economic violence, and child trafficking. It was at this time that I also started blogging about sexual and gender-based violence. Still, this felt inadequate; there was so much more I could do.

In December 2013, I called my parents and informed them of my decision to move back home to start a non-profit organisation. I remember my hands shaking as I grabbed my phone and calculated my words. How would I notify my parents that, without funding or support, I was moving home to start an NGO when I could have a better future abroad? I paced around my room, trying to find the right approach and the right words. Finally, I called my mum. She listened to me and asked if I was sure about my decision. I responded in earnest. It wasn't the complete truth; I was anxious about making a wrong decision and failing. She gave me her blessings and reassured me of her support. It was at that moment that everything changed. With my family's full backing, I felt motivated and reassured.

I anticipated some pushback. I was convinced my village people would plot to pull me down or that my relatives and friends would call for an intervention and try and force me to change my mind. This was me overthinking and suffering from fear of the unknown. It's okay to feel this. The fear of failing or disappointing loved ones can demoralise one but succumbing to it is where defeat begins.

Instead, I received trust, assurance, and the confidence I needed to achieve everything I aimed for. There is something powerful about having the backing of one's family to embark on an advocacy journey. It gives you wings to fly.

Nonetheless, the decision to leave the UN and move back to start advocacy work was a tough decision to make. As a teenager, my life's dream had been to build a career at the UN. I was one step closer to making it come true with the internship. It was like being granted access to the door with no one obstructing you or threatening to shut it. But here I was, about to shut the door to one of the most significant opportunities of my life. Would I ever get such an opportunity again? I didn't have any experience running an NGO, although I had volunteered with one during my National Youth Service Corp mandatory exercise. I felt ill-equipped. What if my NGO flopped? What would I fall back on? Was I making the right decision?

This chapter of my life resonates with the saying "life is a risk." I wouldn't blame anyone reluctant to take such a step; it is only human to hold on to what you have in the face of economic hardship, unemployment, and limited opportunities. All these moments in my life, from the rape, my work at the UN, and the support of my family, motivated me to take that risk. I moved back to Nigeria and founded the Stand to End Rape Initiative (STER)—a feminist-led organisation that implements initiatives to fight the patriarchy and amplify the voices of women and girls.

I remember my first project at STER. I published a call for young Nigerians to join me in protesting sexual violence in Lagos State. I wasn't sure if I would receive any support, but I thought it was worth a shot. As I wore my STER t-shirt and jeans on that day, I was filled with doubt and hope.

It was a new chapter of my life. I was daring to take a stance against violence against women and girls in Nigeria.

My ever-supportive mum patted me on the back and said, "I am proud of you." That was the best form of validation. It gave me the strength I needed to push forward. What amazed me most was the number of young Nigerians who showed up at the protest. Indeed, it takes one person to create a revolution, and I think I did that for Sexual and Gender-based Violence (SGBV) advocacy in Nigeria through STER.

Strategy, Vision, and Impact

STER uses impact measurement systems by monitoring and evaluating long-term positive changes for individuals, communities, and society, resulting from our activities or services. We focus on who we reach, what behaviours have changed, and how well-being has improved. As sexual and gender-based violence is a multifaceted phenomenon, STER addresses this program by applying an ecological lens that focuses on broad-based prevention programming at four levels of the system: individual, relationship, community, and societal.

At the individual level, we focus on addressing personal factors that influence individual behaviour such as gender, age, education, and disabilities. We focus on family, intimate partners, and friends at the relationship level, and in this way address women's empowerment. We focus on neighbourhoods, schools, and workplaces at the community level to address inadequate victim care, weak community sanctions against SGBV, harmful gender roles, and victim-blaming attitudes.

Finally, we focus on broad factors that reduce inhibitions against violence at the societal level, such as economic, social, and gender inequalities, weak legal and criminal justice systems, laws and policies that infringe on women's rights, and social and cultural structures that support violence.

"I call for the criminalization of gender-based violence"
Africa Young Women Beijing+25 Manifesto

One of the most significant impacts of my advocacy thus far has been the passage of the Violence against Persons Prohibition (VAPP),[2] a national law that protects the rights and safety of women in private and public spaces in Nigeria. This law has helped develop the first national sex offenders register in Nigeria. Seeing the smiles on the faces of the women and girls who have received support from STER has been inspiring and encouraging. STER continues to evolve, innovate, and change lives.

The journey hasn't been easy. I remember when I started STER, a Police Public Relations Officer asked why I was wasting my master's degree fighting for women's rights. Why had I left the United Nations to move back to Nigeria to pursue this activism? There were many naysayers who doubted if I could achieve tangible progress through my advocacy. Many didn't believe it was a viable thing to do. Others shamed me for owning my voice and doing something with it. Others only wanted to interact with me because of my violation experience and couldn't see me past being a sexual violence survivor. I was cast as the perfect storytelling victim and invited to relive what had happened to me at public events regardless of the trauma this caused me.

2. https://standtoendrape.org/?portfolio=violence-against-persons-prohibition-bill-vapp

There is something to be said about how feminist activists are expected to perform their trauma in order to validate their work. I stopped accepting such invites. These were difficult times in my journey. I wondered if it was worth it. What carried me through this challenging period was self-belief. It's important to know your purpose, define your vision, and apply your heart to it.

Finding people with a similar vision to join me in my advocacy work has been the most rewarding part. STER went from a one-person idea to an organisation that has attracted nearly two hundred exceptional young Nigerians who understand the vision, have run with it, and contributed to its success today. It is elating and rewarding to be a part of such a community of support.

Self-care, Wellbeing and Mental Health: Lessons Learnt So Far

Notwithstanding, activism doesn't come without its challenges--resources, consistency, and excessive work. There's a constant need to deliver and create change, so much so that we forget to respond to our body's need for rest. Our body sensations sometimes tell us we are "not doing enough." I have moments of self-doubt where I focus on how much I have not achieved. There is a thin line between self-motivation and burnout. There is that general innate fear of missing or losing out or becoming irrelevant when one is not visibly attending important conferences, being granted speaking engagements or winning awards. This is a valid fear but remember that your purpose has no expiry date and He who has sent you is everlasting. Rest is a worthy sacrifice. I was burning out and hiding from responding to emails or speaking invitations. For about two years, I turned down 95% of the invitations that came my way, not because they did not align with my passion, but more for the sake of managing the fatigue and burnout I felt.

One essential thing I do for myself now is to tune off. I do not need to be seen or heard because I have achieved a lot for myself and need my rest.

"Even Jesus rested on the seventh day. Oluwaseun Ayodeji Osowobi, rest in Jesus' name," I always say to myself jokingly.

I am disciplined with caring for my well-being as I know that if I fail to rest, I cannot fulfill the work of my Father. I lean into my faith in Christ and speak the word of God that addresses strength and claim them to reality. As a smarter activist today, my work-life balance is essential to me. I must prioritise my well-being to continue to support and create spaces for others.

Creating Spaces

I continue to create spaces for African women within the international community. Some have viewed this as tokenism. I, on the other hand, view such opportunities as key to building inclusivity, creating stepping stones, and giving more visibility to the work that is being done by an admirable cohort of young African women. It's important to bring other African voices into global spaces and continue to grow and thrive in the spirit of **Ubuntu**.

The Africa We Want Is
"A prosperous Africa based on inclusive
growth and sustainable development"
African Union Agenda 2063

There were occasions when I was shut out from accessing opportunities and funding, so my mantra has become to support other young people and provide them with the support I lacked but later found.

As a young woman navigating feminism, I have found that young feminist organising is essential because of our shared struggles and concerns. Feminism encourages women to support each other to end sexism. My introduction to feminism started with my mum. I witnessed how she supported her sisters, consciously and consistently found opportunities to thrive, and achieved great economic heights. This has shaped my activism, where my work is to uplift the voices and needs of other African women and girls.

As an African woman, my struggles have different folds: oppression, oppressors, and enablers. Oppressive social and cultural practices have been reinforced over time, whether it has to do with inefficient policies, institutions, gender norms, or biases. Such practices perpetuate the vicious cycle of prioritising men's liberty and freedom while caging women's rights and voices. The battles we fight today are not new, but they take different forms in today's world: gender-pay gap, access to STEM spaces, and sexual and gender-based violence, to name a few. Looking into the future, my hope is for a society that embraces the existence of women and girls and respects them; a society that has space for them as equals deserving of opportunities, just like their male counterparts. That is where the older generation has stopped; we may proceed and achieve an equitable and just society for African women and girls.

The path that leads to making a difference is sometimes crooked, complicated, and confusing; stay on the course. Be determined, diligent, and dogged. Every activism starts with a story; what is yours and what change are you creating with it?

CHAPTER FIVE

Reproductive Justice Is Always the Last Frontier
Reproductive Justice, Between Taboos and Freedom
by Ms. Rosebell Kagumire

"I am Nala
because I confront silences and
silencing"

I was born in 1983, just a little over twenty years after Uganda's independence. The war that would later bring to power the current and longest-serving president, Yoweri Museveni, was raging. Uganda was a country forcibly constructed through British, Belgian, and German colonisation in Eastern and Central Africa, which resulted in the breaking up of dozens of indigenous African nations. At that point, post-independent Uganda was reeling from the worst military regime of Idi Amin and a deeply divided times-of-independence leader, Dr. Apollo Milton Obote. It was a fragile period, as the political elite and military men were fighting to control and dictate how to piece together what had been dismantled by the colonial system, sidelining the intellectual prowess and efforts of ordinary people that had been instrumental in attaining independence. The immediate post-colonial period was also about attempting to circumvent the neo-colonial strategies that were being rolled out as former colonial powers rebranded themselves through proxy and shadow political organisations.

Post Idi Amin, the country had remained divided. Elections in 1980 were largely seen as illegitimate, leading to various political and military splinter groups. It was from this period that Museveni and his colleagues emerged with military might. If you hadn't escaped the country, life for many who had barely made sense of the loss of lives, trauma, and economic strife under Amin was bleak.

My parents went to school during Idi Amin's dictatorship. My mother's diploma ceremony hung in our living room for years. In it, she is shaking the big hands of Idi Amin. This is inscribed in my mind as a reminder that it wasn't so long ago.

NalaFem

The 1970's and 80s are still talked about in Uganda, not only because of the mass killings and excesses of militarism that occurred, but also because the country's economy collapsed and many families, including my parents, could hardly afford household items like soap and salt. Black markets ruled as Uganda was isolated regionally.

In 1986, Museveni came into power through a coup. A big part of the country was under the control of his forces except for the north and northeastern parts of the country. I spent my adolescent years in the 90s in southwestern Uganda where, for the first time in twenty years, there was a semblance of peace. However, it would take another twenty years for Uganda's north and eastern people to glimpse that peace. They faced one of the most devastating wars in post-independent Uganda. Ugandans in these regions spent these twenty years in internally displaced peoples' camps and experienced the enormous loss of families and dignity, as well as killings, displacement, hunger, and subjugation by both the government and rebel groups like the Lord's Resistance Army (LRA).

Although I did not live in a region where there was war, the legacies of colonialism, neocolonialism, and post-independence wars were a reality in my childhood. Our families struggled to afford education and health care. As a result, I was always aware of what I was privileged to access and what I was denied. I was privileged to live in a peaceful place given all the mayhem and struggle for political control that the country was still going through. In all these phases, the formal and informal ways of educating young people had been eroded.

Families were separated for safety, schools were dilapidated, and teachers' salaries disappeared.

If a parent was to get their child a good education, the boarding school system was the best option. The boarding school system was introduced by the colonial rulers and was brought on as the best choice at the time, for it was deemed necessary to separate children from their families in order to make them "educated." Therefore, at thirteen years of age, just like my parents had done before, I was sent to boarding school to pursue my secondary education.

It is important to understand the broader context behind the practice of boarding schools in the British colonial system and the pivotal role they played as they sought to shape African children's outlook of the empire and the world. In colonial Uganda, boarding schools had been used as a space to impart western civilisation on African children. These children were taken away from home to institutions headed mostly by white teachers who would ensure that there was not much semblance of "Africanness" in them by the time they left school.

Although we are now independent, the legacy of boarding schools continues today. Just like me, after the age of ten and increasingly even younger, many children in Uganda spend their lives in institutional care—boarding schools—visiting their own homes every three months for a three-week break. In colonial times, being taught by white teachers was a defining indicator of class and prestige. At a time when children were denied education if their parents didn't accept being Christianised, being taught by white missionaries symbolised one's closeness to white power—the status quo. It was meant to lead you on a path of entering the "who is who" in the colony.

This legacy of the colonial practice of boarding schools continues in different circumstances and for different reasons. However, it still fosters the continued separation of children from families during a crucial stage of development—adolescence.

In African culture, preparing a child for adulthood was a poignant moment and a crucial process. It was a duty that family and community embraced and carried. Transitioning to adulthood was not expected to be a lonely journey. It was a community journey with ceremonies.

The Africa We Want Is
"An Africa with a strong cultural identity,
common heritage, values and ethics"
African Union Agenda 2063

Entire nations and communities today still have fragments of these ceremonies, which survived colonial erasure. These ceremonies prepare an adolescent for adulthood. Apart from large communal rituals, the family's daily teaching was expected to impart in a child an understanding of their body and what was coming ahead. With some flaws, of course, African and indigenous communities had ways of knowing that were passed on through daily and ceremonial practices. For instance, in many Bantu-speaking communities in East Africa, a paternal aunt or uncle was an entire institution tasked with cultural memorialisation and passing on of sex education, exploring pleasure, and sexual politics to teenagers—both girls and boys. Some communities still uphold this practice. The roles played by an aunt or uncle are still embraced in my community and are most visible during marriage ceremonies.

With school systems firmly in place taking up most of the children's time, one would think some of that education would be imparted by the school, but this has not been the case. I always flashback to my first days of boarding school, especially when conversations about children and education, and how our society ill-treats girls, arise. I remember crying as my mom and her friend dropped me off in the mid-afternoon and the car exited the school gate. It was not too terrifying as other students from my home village were in the same school. In addition, the school was only some twenty-five kilometres from home. Nevertheless, there was a feeling of being abandoned, and no one prepares you for that feeling.

Just yesterday, I had been a child, my parents waking me up and supervising my morning preschool routine. And then boom, here I was entirely on my own, navigating a new world. Creating new friends was no longer done at one's whim but out of a need to survive this new environment.

There was not a lot of specialised sex education in the school curriculum or as part of extracurricular activities. In a country where more than half the schools have a religious foundation and rely on public funding, the education system struggles to separate organised religion from education. Schools accept or reject what can be taught formally and informally based on "religious morality." However, at my boarding school, we received some primary science education. We also had a school matron you could approach if you were not feeling well. Much of sex education, therefore, was informal and peer-to-peer.

Our dormitory was organised with four students sharing two double-decker beds with a space in between.

In the third and last term of the year, I finally gathered the courage to ask one of the girls what a period felt like. She had a quiet humour about her. She realised that, at thirteen years old, no one had told me anything about periods, save for the rushed reproduction lessons our male science teacher had given us back in primary school, to the chuckles of both girls and boys. She gave me a crash course on menstrual hygiene and told me not to be afraid if and when it happened. I was in school growing up away from my parents, and no one was there to guide me through what to expect of my body.

For many, the information came from peers and myths often exchanged in hushed voices as girls waited for "lights out" at night. We were away from the watchful eyes of aunties and family. If you came from a home with struggling parents, as most of us did, you knew girls' education beyond primary school was not always a given. Hence, we felt and knew we were lucky to be in this school.

Still, I was privileged that my maternal grandfather was a teacher and made sure my mother got an education. All my grandparents revered education; those who hadn't got far in school worked hard to see their children go farther than them. Many women in both families had been educated past lower secondary school. I never felt I would be denied an education because of my gender. All this put me in a better place, right from my village to my school.

But being in school and not being taught about your own body, and being at home where academic excellence was the only thing a teenager's mind was supposed to be dealing with, was not easy. Family and society insinuated that as a girl, you understood your parents' sacrifices well enough not to "fool around."

Any mistake or sexual activity could end your dreams! This was the threat wielded at home and in school, all without educating girls on how to prevent that from happening.

It was during the holidays that my first period arrived. I didn't talk about it with anyone. I remember feeling such excruciating pain. It was challenging to get sanitary pads in a rural area and even though my mother could have tightened her budget and gotten them, she was away for work. I finally opened up to my cousin, who shared her supplies. In the following days when the shared supplies ran out, I had to improvise. My cousin advised me to tell my mother, but I remember thinking, how do you start a conversation about something held so secretly that elders never really talk about it?

It was during my "going back to school" shopping, when I added the pads to my shopping list, that my mother found out I needed them and had started my period. It was clear this would be treated as another need my mother had to fulfill, but no serious conversation about it would follow. It was a relief not to have to talk about it much, but it also left me wondering what it was I didn't know.

Looking back, it really is unbelievable that neither our parents nor our teachers were equipped to speak candidly to children about their changing bodies, an experience that millions of young girls go through while their bodies remain shrouded in secrecy. I didn't talk about periods with an adult or what this stage of my life meant in school or at home. As teens, we relied on information from older students or older cousins who passed on their knowledge, including how to practice menstrual hygiene.

While our puzzlement united us, the information shared, especially regarding sex, was never entirely factual, clothed as it was in socialisations and myths about what a woman's body was about and the gender roles around sex as a practice. But who was there to sieve the correct from the incorrect? No one.

At the age of fourteen, in my second year of secondary school, I changed schools. We were summoned into an abrupt meeting in the first three weeks back at our all-girls school. We were all to go to the "sick bay" in the school healthcare unit. There we found doctors and nurses from outside the school. I remember the nervous murmurs and the fear that some students felt. This was the first exercise of forced pregnancy testing. We would go through this for five more years. We were confused because the mandatory pregnancy checks did not teach any of us girls what to do. All we knew were a list of phrases yelled at us at home by relatives if they saw or suspected you had been talking to a boy— "noyiija kusisikara" (you will get spoiled), as if one was a glass of milk. No one was ever willing to share a drop of knowledge and create a space to educate and empower us, not at home and not at school.

The unwritten rule was an expectation that adolescents do not engage in sex. Based on the moral judgement taught in church and the random warnings by relatives, it was hoped that you got enough sense to stay away from danger. Even with the ever-present danger of sexual abuse, the conversation always placed responsibility on the teenage girl to ensure she and anyone outside her did nothing to or with her body.

During the holidays, teenage girls had sex with little sex education and not much access to contraception. The act was risky. Instead of education, the forced pregnancy tests—a blatant violation of our little bodies and our privacy—was seen as the best option to send a message. One or two unlucky girls ended up getting pregnant sometimes. The whole school knew because their parents were called to take them out of school. These one or two cases of confirmed pregnancy were used as a tool to threaten other girls from having sex. None of the "educated adults" stopped to question this humiliation and the impulse to punish a pregnant girl without understanding her circumstances. Expulsion and humiliation were shown as punishment and used to set an example for other young girls. Pregnancy was put before the few girls lucky to access secondary education as the dealbreaker without any sympathy and support.

"I call for ending gender descrimination"
Africa Young Women Beijing+25
Manifesto

One girl in my year got pregnant and was expelled. I remember the violence of it well. There were no second chances. One couldn't be allowed to come back if they had a baby; there was never a conversation about whether the girl had been violated or not— many girls were in "relationships" with adults. No one cared if it was rape.

The irony was that once the fear had died down and the girls were expelled from school, our night stories back in the dormitories were often about our boyfriends. Many of my friends' debut sex experiences came early.

I used to live vicariously through their stories—some were exaggerated, of course; you could tell there was this desire to be seen as "knowing men." I was always in awe and a little bit jealous of one friend who enjoyed sex with her boyfriend at fifteen, an age when many of us were still gripped by fear. She would share her many sex stories. During those times when the internet was yet to come to us, problematic romance novels—Mills & Boon and others—reigned. We would devour the few we could get our hands on. They were some kind of contraband in school. Looking back, these books, with their white characters, painted a picture of desirability that was unreachable for girls like me. Without much exposure to television, these books were already shaping how we viewed ourselves and what others should find attractive in us. Long hair for women, big built chests for men, blue or brown eyes—these books took up so much space describing characters whom we'd never met and who didn't look like us or anyone we knew.

Surprisingly, these experiences happened in parallel with the fear-based sex talk and messaging dispensed by the school and at home. The HIV/AIDS epidemic was used to threaten and deter young people from having sex. Almost all of us had someone close, a relative or a neighbour, who had died of an AIDS-related illness or was battling it. Without much treatment available in our countries or even money to access the expensive treatment, the suffering of those who got infected was unbearable to watch. Abstinence-from-sex messaging was seen as the right tool with which to target teenagers.

Yet here we were late into the night in dormitories sharing stories of our sexual experiences, which were either pleasant or abusive.

NalaFem

Counsellors came to "instil morals" and preformed scary AIDS dramas, but these never tamed the stories amongst us about teenage sex and relationship dramas. Of course, there was also the slut-shaming that followed girls who were thought to be sexually active, or girls who were demonstrably unafraid of their sexuality and spoke openly about it. There we were, growing into adults literally on our own.

Often, adult men took advantage of and abused underage girls. If you got pregnant, you could be forced to marry. Some of the most brilliant girls and women I knew dropped out of school because they fell pregnant and never got the chance to return. So, even though no one had explained to me what a period was or how to navigate adolescence, I was warned constantly by parents, relatives, and other adults not to be like "so and so."

I must have been about sixteen when my mom found out I had a boyfriend. I was scared to death because this was not expected. This kind of fear made most of us teenagers relate in ways our parents never had a clue about. We had relationships we couldn't talk about because of the fear of HIV and pregnancy shared with us everyday by our elders. This left no room to look at teenagers as growing sexual beings who needed guidance.

This unwritten rule that as a teen, your body is not yours and whatever you do with it must be hidden is still the norm. If you came from a life of struggle like me—where school fees came almost at the expense of your parents' sanity— the fear of disappointing them would run your life. My parents, particularly my mother, was struggling to raise school fees for six children. Sports helped keep me focused and shielded me from boredom while also distracting me from many body image issues that teenagers experience.

NalaFem

The flip side of it was that sports, and the stereotypes associated with femininity, influenced how peers around me saw me. I felt they saw me as not sexual. It would take me up to my twenties to really relate to my body and embody my sexuality.

Looking back on the experience of living for three months with hundreds of other young teens in just a few hectares of fenced land makes me wonder how we survived all that. Could we have been something else if our spirits and bodies hadn't been constrained within those wire fences?

The idea that sex is for adults is disturbing given how society puts the price of its negligence on little bodies and lives. I do not remember anyone checking in on me, a friendly check-in to see if I felt safe or if I had life questions outside my academic performance. This is still a reality for many children. In our communities, we survived attempted sexual assaults that we could never talk about with anyone in our family; for some children, this abuse took place right inside the school, which was supposed to be a safe space. We made it out of those years, but some girls didn't. From discontinued education to early marriages and abortion-related deaths, these things happened to girls I knew, loved, friended, and communed with.

Today's struggles

It took me years to find spaces and time to reflect on these issues. The path to my social justice work has opened up space for me to dedicate my time and resources to others. The critical understanding of my personal lived experiences and how they relate to the prevailing social realities has been crucial to this work. My feminist journey demands that I reflect on my lived experiences—what went well, where was I privileged, where was I abused even when I might not have seen it as abuse at the time.

Often, the school environment comes to mind. The detachment between school and home, what home thinks school is supposed to teach you and what school offers, leaves a glaring gap that fails so many girls on our continent.

My interest in women's liberation on this continent comes from deeper conversations with myself that force me to contend with what justice could look like for the next generation. We can have the right to education, the right to work, the right to vote; we can have women presidents and even be proudly shown off as pioneers in fields where women and girls were denied entry for such a long time. But without ensuring that our bodies belong to us right from childhood, all these rights are built on sand.

"I champion gender equality"
United Nations Sustainable Development Goals

The current struggles to deny adolescents and teenagers sexuality education are too painful to watch. For many young people, the school is yet to be reimagined and reformed as a safe place that can prepare them to face life's complex realities. As the push for more children to access schools progresses and we see gender gaps closing in primary and lower secondary school, so must support for the young people reclaiming their voice on body politics, sexuality education, gender, and sexuality. Young people's movements are already shaping the present and future of our continent. An average citizen in Africa is around twenty years old.

This is a reflection from my adolescent years on what could change and how we can pave the way for a more just and healthier world and ensure that millions of young African people do not have to live through the same circumstances we lived through, two decades later.

NalaFem

CHAPTER SIX

Shedding The Fear of Justifying Our Lives
by Ms. Rose Wachuka Macharia

"I am Nala
because the collectivity of our voices
and actions emboldens me to become
the future we seek for women and girls"

A Stubbornly Curious Child...

There is much from my childhood that I clearly recall. I remember walking to primary school through a village rich with the scent of burnt pounded maize (ugali). I wondered why my mother did not make us Ugali--the starch-packed delicacy Kenyans usually have for breakfast. I remember dreading lunchtime because my meals were different from the green maize and potato mix that my classmates brought to school. I also remember how I used to go to school with shoes on while most of my classmates came barefoot. I tried to hide my shoes and share my lunch. Sometimes, I would hide it and pretend that I, too, ate pounded maize for breakfast. I often struggled with status. I felt the need to belong. I felt a strong urge to minimise and shutter inequalities. This was my youthful notion of justice—an idea that would become central in my life and career.

I grew up in a family of five children. All my siblings are boys and I am tucked in the middle. Throughout my childhood, I had deep questions about our separation of chores, about the more sensitive and heightened attention I received from my father and about the constrained energy I observed my mother confine--a brilliant physicist and mathematician who still needed the approval of her husband to wear trousers. A bold woman who until the 90s surrendered her entire salary to her husband and consumed only what was surrendered to her. A beautifully vivacious spirit who for close to a decade of gainful employment did not earn the right to housing allowance, which was enjoyed by my father, even though she, like my father, was also a teacher.

I have spent a lot of time reflecting about my notions of justice. I recognised that because of these experiences, my attention and sensitivities to gender justice became heightened at a very young age. I noticed when women were subjected to support roles and when their contributions were ignored. I noticed the way teachers treated female students who did well in class compared to our male counterparts. My earliest encounter with justice was centred on gender justice and it formed the basis of my activism in my early adult years.

Based on these experiences, I started to construct my life story. I was seven years old then with a vision clear as day of how my life was supposed to pan out. I was going to be known for my articulation of things that affected humanity. I was going to support my family through the social strata and make our home the envy of many. I was going to marry a doctor who would ride motorcycles and win championships. Together, we would travel the world, adopt children, and never age. I had an active and vivid mind.

My parents got married very young. By the time my mother attained the age of thirty and my father thirty-two, we had all been born. At that time, VCR machines and coloured television were making their debut into the African market. My father was a gadgets man. So, he purchased a set for business and leisure. He recorded music and movies on Video Home System (VHS) tapes and operated a cinema. Much of my childhood social learnings, beliefs and moral inclinations were therefore drawn from and harnessed from these movies. I was building personal character and a mental profile. Besides my immediate family experiences and the experiences from school, new media and entertainment were heavy influencers.

But they all had the greatest effect on my constructed understanding, approach and sensitivities around masculinity and gender justice.

I recall a film that my family loved—Nam Angels. The plot was centred on American motorcycle outlaws on jungle bikes moving into Vietnam to rescue a colleague from an ex-Nazi's tribe. This film, which was a family favourite, left a gnawing dissatisfaction in my mind about how it featured women and how this affected me and my social interactions. My brothers each adopted a character against whom they mirrored their behaviour when we played the shooting game. There were no women in the film after whom I could mirror my tactics for the shooting game. The film did not feature strong female characters. So, I filled the gaps as I deemed fit. I imagined myself as a soldier, fighting side by side with these heroes, commanding, directing and emerging with my autonomy, freedom and authenticity, intact.

The reversal of this reality of minimising women in culture and the arts gave rise to my public writing about justice and human dignity. It also inspired a movement, The Voice of Women Initiative (VOW-I), which consolidated women's voices around the world and amplified them on a platform that allowed celebration and recognition. Fellow activists Aya Chebbi, Delphine Konda, and I called it a platform that recognised ordinary women doing extraordinary things. We were nominated for the Hero Goody Award in 2013 as a result of this initiative's impact. We also introduced VOW-I at the DW Global Media Forum and inspired gender consciousness in news and film. It also gave rise to a decadelong advocacy on balanced gender casting, representation, and celebration.

I wanted to make sure girls had a broader cultural education than the closed class of only male stardom depicted by this and many other films today. I am still pursuing, directly and through multiple other channels, the importance and centrality of women as lead characters in film, in culture, and in the arts.

I also pushed boundaries, sometimes forcefully. I knew that things would work out if I pushed beyond the stubborn voice in my head that reminded me to tone myself down and defer to others, who were often older, more popular or more confident than I was.

I remember feeling the need to belong to an older generation, even at Nyandarua High School where I spent my early years scrutinising student life. I was in awe of the ease with which most students went about daily chores. My nostrils remember pupils at Nyandarua High school smelling like broken oranges mixed with budding lavender and shredded lemongrass falling on thirsty earth. That scent became my memory of adulthood. I knew that if high school was my gateway to the freedoms that being an adult brought, then I would certainly not miss the chance.

May I Please...

We always shot up when the teacher walked into class.

Next was a chorus that went something like this, "Good morning, teacher... May we please sit-down, teacher?" A simple request to go to the toilet could be refused by the teacher. One would walk up to the teacher and whisper, "Please, teacher, may I go to the toilet?" The answer was often a reprimanding order for the student concerned to stay put until the end of the lesson. This happened to me during a science lesson in class five. It was Mrs. Mbela's class.

She was a stern stickler for discipline and a teacher whose duty weeks gave me sleepless nights because she would cane us on both hands when we arrived late at school.

My brother Peter and I were often late because we had to walk three kilometres from home in Chaka to the bus stop, and then hope that we would find transportation to King'ong'o in Nyeri twelve kilometers away. Nobody ever asked how we got to school. Nobody knew that we had to wake up at 4:30am to try and make it to school before 7.00am. Nobody cared. So, when Mrs. Mbela denied me permission to take a call of nature, it made me cry.

About a decade later, I thought about that experience and cringed. Having to seek permission for even the most basic things had far-reaching effects—even in my adult life. In Pedagogy of the Oppressed, Paulo Freire observes that "the oppressed, having internalised the image of the oppressor and adopted his guidelines, are fearful of freedom." Asking for permission was all I knew. It made me feel obedient. It made me feel responsible. It made me feel deserving. What I did not realise was that it had also numbed my capacity to question indignifying actions. Eventually, I overcame the fear of standing up for myself and for others. Today, I defend people who do not have the power to defend themselves. This is my life's calling.

"I call for access to justice and protection"
Africa Young Women Beijing+25 Manifesto

I spent the next twenty years of my life detesting the culture of waiting to be allowed to do anything. When I look back on those permission-seeking years, I find consonance between the embedded "ethos of discipline" that school purported to instil and the colonial tools of control.

It was apparent to my budding mind that we were being set up for a life of direction, stagnation, dependence, and control. I knew that if I was to explore all the parts of me that bore freedom and exceptionality, I had to allow my mind to ignore the voice of subjugation programmed into it by formal and informal systems of learning. I learnt a lot through observation. Because I was often too isolated from my peers, I learnt more from our home's keeper than I did at school.

I often found myself alone, unable to fit in at school or at home. In the course of spending time with Nyambura, the housekeeper, I remember being bothered deeply by religion and the practices that I observed around me. I once went to an overnight prayer event with our housekeeper. I must have been six. Troubled by the way worshippers were "shaken" by the spirit, I spent many daylight hours staring into the clouds hoping to have a conversation with the forces that occupied the universe and that were so powerful worshippers became incoherent in their presence. I questioned my own "goodness" because I could not power my prayers to bring me such trembling force. I looked for insights in books, in friends, and in nature. Today, I know that the power within me is greater than any unknown and unseen.

In The Footsteps of My Grandfather

Kenya's struggle for freedom was not a diplomatic affair. In 1952, the Mau Mau uprising, a nationalist movement organised to resist British rule in Kenya and fight for land, sparked a historic freedom movement that forever changed the trajectory of the justice system in Kenya.

My maternal grandfather, Mathenge wa Njari, then one of a handful of educated Kenyans, joined the battle. His efforts earned him seven years in detention in Manda, an Island in Lamu along Kenya's Indian Ocean coast and in Mfangano, an island on Lake Victoria in Kenya's city of Kisumu, then known as Port Victoria. My grandfather was a successful businessman who traded in alcohol and other consumer goods and who owned businesses in the busy towns of Nanyuki and Karatina. He was a freedom fighter who joined the war for independence because he believed that Africans could take charge of their national affairs and self-govern.

He met my grandmother in 1964, a kind-hearted fair-skinned woman with two young girls aged one and three, whose work ethic and radiating beauty immediately caught his attention. He married her as a second wife. That is how my mother, the older of the two girls, became his daughter. The other girl was my aunt, Mukami.

Although he was educated, my grandfather's level of exposure and the nature of his upbringing did not prepare him to raise two fiercely independent and intelligent girls whose brilliance was unconcealable. They quickly assumed notoriety for their stellar performance in academics. My grandfather had other priorities besides ensuring that my mother and aunt were educated. When it became apparent to my grandmother that their education was not of any concern to her husband, she sought help from her brother, my grandfather Tumuti. He provided basic support by paying for their primary education while my grandmother worked tirelessly to cover their post-primary education needs, including their college tuition.

My mother taught mathematics and physics before her retirement in November 2020. At Nyandarua High School, students made fun of us by saying that our food was prepared using physics formulas. It therefore baffled me why she had not pursued a science or engineering course at the university. Her brilliance amazed me. Although my grandfather loved me dearly, as I did him, his decision not to prioritise my mother and aunt Mukami's education registered in my mind as neglect on account of gender. It created an urge in my heart and mind to break every thread of patriarchy in my own life and in the lives of as many women as I possibly could.

My mother's dream was to become a lawyer. I inherited it as my own and committed myself to becoming a great jurist. I was seven when I made that promise. I attribute my earnest need for justice to the marginalisation I observed in the lives of the women closest to me. Paradoxically, even though I admired my grandfather's contribution to the freedom struggle, I was fuelled by a deep desire to reverse his prejudicial denial of my mother's education.

All Are Equal Before the Law

My father and grandfather had a strained relationship because for many years, my father had failed to meet his traditional obligations regarding dowry. I found my father's stance liberating and saw it as a chance to defy future expectations of myself. Among the Kikuyu, a father could not accept dowry unless he had fulfilled the obligation towards his own wife. My young mind found the opportunity to decide what traditions applied to me deliciously liberating. My father, indirectly, was offering me the opportunity to determine this course for myself.

I am sometimes convinced that my father, by breaking this chain of dowry negotiations, was freeing me from its expectations.

"I champion peace, justice and strong institutions" *United Nations Sustainable Development Goals*

The 2010 Constitution of Kenya enshrined justice for all in stipulating that married or unmarried, all can be equal beneficiaries of ancestral property. The utility of dowry and its implications on inheritance, burial rites and acceptance has decreased over time although society, stubbornly, continues to fight back. I am braced for this battle as I have been throughout my career. I often think about the opportunities that are denied women and girls by patriarchal beliefs and practices. The unspoken truth is that our entrenched patriarchal culture encumbers us greatly.

For as long I can remember, I have had an insatiable desire to accomplish things beyond my own expectations. As a little girl raised alongside four boys, I related success with masculinity because that is what I witnessed being celebrated. I have been referred to as intense, high octane, and aggressive by both men and women. Because these words have not been meant as compliments, I have found myself attempting to be "softer." Although I have decided to allow myself to develop a public profile, I still feel the shackles of insecurity and the voices of online critics pulling me back. The consequence is that I have a string of accomplishments nobody really knows anything about.

Yet, I am stronger emotionally and socially because I have invested a great deal of time to build my confidence and shed the lessons of timidity I was handed as a child. I have now embraced my femininity and am proud of it.

I see being female being celebrated and the accomplishments of women documented for all to see. Now more than ever, women must become comfortable with expressing their deep value. We must own our accomplishments and dive deeply into ourselves to untie the chords of otherness that hold us back from owning our contributions on this planet. Although the situation greatly improves with each generation, there still remain interests that threaten the ability of women to fully thrive in a fair and equal world.

If Opportunity Doesn't Knock, Build a Door

Modern societies re-package sexism in ways that intimidate women and prevent them from fully owning their stories. This is akin to what was seen in the past. In the field of law, Mary Beard, the classic feminist writer, illustrates this "same forest – different species" approach using the stories of three women in ancient Rome whose natural conditions failed to keep them silent. The first, Maesia, successfully defended herself in the Courts and, characterised as having masculine traits, was called an androgyne. Afrania, the second, initiated legal cases on her own behalf and was imprudent enough to plead in person, so that everyone became tired with her "barking" and "yapping" (she was not allowed human speech). The only information available about her is the year of her death—48BC—because it was more important to record when she died than what she accomplished. However, the third, Hortensia, is more uplifted in Roman history because she always spoke in defence of her children, husband, and other women.

I recognise these three women and the prejudices they endured in the lives of women I have encountered in my personal and professional lives. Examples of this can be seen in modern day East Africa.

A confident and competent female Minister is often referred to as "the only man in cabinet." This is because a woman speaking in public is still, structurally and by subtle aggression, not considered a woman. This need to suppress women's voices and agency is hardwired into our culture, religion and history, and, though it will take many more years to effectively solve the problem, we each must rise to the challenge.

I cannot claim for certain that women will stop being derailed and maligned, but I do know that the pain felt by women today will protect others in the future. History is awash with stories of women who have borne the wrath of patriarchal societies by going against well-articulated and widely accepted norms. African women such as Sarah Baartman were paraded across cities because of the amusement their bodies brought to many in western societies. In the United Kingdom, the suffragists were threatened, tortured, and tormented for the audacity to call for equal voting rights. In Kenya, women were ostracised for daring into political spaces and for pursuing the equal rights of matrimony and property.

I have watched versions of marginalisation throughout my life. There is Maesia, represented by the insults hurled against Former First Lady of the United States, Michelle Obama, who is one of the most inspiring figures in all of history. There is Afrania, represented in the realities of many women who have dared to challenge unjust laws and customs. There is Hortensia, represented in the life of my mother, whose courage is despised by an extended family whose idea of justice does not include women at its helm.

NalaFem

The collective resolve of these and many other women further destroys the macro and micro aggressions visited upon women every millisecond of every day. As the saying goes, "no pain, no gain." In addition to re-examining our understanding of the "voice of authority," we must think more about the fault lines and fractures that underlie dominant male discourse.

Power is still considered to be the domain of men. Through the digital sphere, we can challenge these norms by stubbornly elevating the image of authority as also belonging to women everywhere. Confidence is a key ally in realising this objective, which is within reach. The confidence to communicate one's accomplishments is extremely valuable.

My identity as a leader has often called these experiences into introspection. When we look to the past and see the strides that have been made, the equality debate becomes easier. As we continue to occupy more spaces of power and leadership, justice and protection become possible.

The Law as a Companion Towards Freedom

At age seventeen, I watched the Kenyan Judicial Commission of Inquiry into the Goldenberg Affair with near obsession. The Goldenberg scandal was a political scandal in which the Kenyan government was found to have subsidised exports of gold far beyond standard arrangements during the 1990s. The government did this by paying the company Goldenberg International 35% more (in Kenyan shillings) than their foreign currency earnings. Although it notionally appears that the scheme was intended to earn hard currency for the country, it is estimated to have cost Kenya the equivalent of more than 10% of the country's annual gross domestic product, and it is possible that no or minimal amounts of gold were actually exported.

NalaFem

I remember marvelling at Advocates Gibson Kamau Kuria, Agnes Murgor (now Judge of Appeal and a dear friend), and Waweru Gatonye's mastery of the proceedings. I recall thinking that courtroom advocacy provided the most untethered and unfettered avenue for self-expression. In court, I could assume a full range of expression under the cover of justice, for myself and for those whose causes I happened to be championing.

Privately, I decided I would pursue law. Like many parents, mine had decided that a career in pharmacy was the best fit for me. I did not argue, though I made a pact with myself that the law would be my chosen companion. Only later would I realise that the principles I so passionately pursued were justice and human dignity. In line with my yearning to find freedom for myself and others, I came to consider a fulfilling life to be one which prioritises the human existence as it is, without the burdens of class, status or constructed stations of life. A life that anchors belonging as the existence of the human race and all the rights and freedoms that accompany that existence.

A deeper belief in this idea would later be catalysed by an incident I witnessed on my way back from work in 2013. I was walking through Ng'ando Village in Dagoretti Constituency in Nairobi when I saw a woman sprawled on the dusty road. She looked like she was in her mid-forties or thereabouts. She was writhing in pain and her dress was up to her waist, exposing her under garments. She was screaming while pulling her braids out of her hair. A crowd surrounded her, clearly shocked by her misery, exchanging murmurs and speculating about the cause of her pain. Someone said it was witchcraft.

I remember marvelling at Advocates Gibson Kamau Kuria, Agnes Murgor (now Judge of Appeal and a dear friend), and Waweru Gatonye's mastery of the proceedings. I recall thinking that courtroom advocacy provided the most untethered and unfettered avenue for self-expression. In court, I could assume a full range of expression under the cover of justice, for myself and for those whose causes I happened to be championing.

It later turned out that she had a serious case of meningitis, a condition that would have been fatal had she not been taken to the hospital in time. I wrote about this experience on my blog, *The Green Background*, under the title "I vote for Health." I had a strong resolve that good leadership prioritises the most intimate needs of people, including healthcare. That day, I had an epiphany: justice without dignity is incomplete. Armed with these values, I chose to pursue a career in Government.

In 2011, I joined the Kenyan Bar as an Advocate of the High Court of Kenya. I had made the decision to carve a niche for myself in constitution and public interest litigation. I chose Waweru Gatonye as my pupil master because he was a respected jurist who valued brilliance, innovation, and depth in a young mind. Together, we established a constitutional law practice that has become one of the most consulted law firms in Kenya, contributing greatly to the evolution of the cardinal principles of constitutional interpretation in the legal regime of the country in the period following the promulgation of the Constitution of Kenya 2010.

Our approach was aimed at developing social justice jurisprudence. The Kenyan Constitution, in its values, principles and rules, reflects the desire by Kenyans to break with our country's unequal and authoritarian past and forge a different path towards democracy and egalitarianism.

The pronouncement in the preamble to the Constitution's Article 10 on the values and principles of national governance, and Article 19 on the purpose of the Bill of Rights, all lead to the conclusion that the Constitution is a *charter for social transformation*.

The concept of social or sociological jurisprudence (as it is most known), was first elaborated by Roscoe Pound, a prolific writer and Dean of the Harvard Law School in 1911. The idea was to examine the social effects of legal institutions, doctrines, and opinions. The principle examines the social aspect of law, evaluating the sociological effects on substantive and procedural law. It stresses that the practical aspect of law and, in fact, the very function of law, is to satisfy the maximum number of people and resolve conflicts among individuals in society.

This movement of sociological jurisprudence emerged in the era of progressive development, which Pound termed "a movement for pragmatism as a philosophy of law," with the purpose to create legal reforms and through these, social change. Whereas formal jurisprudence employed the logic of specific assumed principles of precedence, social jurisprudence advocated for the use of social sciences to develop legal rules, arguing for freedom for Judges to seek justice on a case-by-case basis. Through the Constitution, this approach has been instrumentalised, giving Judges and Judicial Officers decisional autonomy.

During my nascent legal career at the firm of Waweru Gatonye Advocates, those who retained our advice sought constitutional interpretation on interests secured during the practice of an all-powerful Executive. I wanted to thrive in an ecosystem that allowed me to defend the Constitution and explore the principles of justice without leaning on jurisprudence and legal practice that focused justification on a scarred legal past.

Aware of the transitional tensions between an authoritarian past and a broadly democratic and empowering future, and the deep-seated interests represented in this tension, my solution was to join the Judiciary.

Being the final custodian and guarantor of the Constitution, the Judiciary has the burden of providing jurisprudential leadership for the country and developing a uniquely Kenyan jurisprudence that balances individual rights, group rights and collective interests, which resonates with the desire of Kenyans for a *socially just state and society*. Specifically, the broad contours of such *social justice jurisprudence* would involve firm and bold enforcement of human, social and economic rights, and the equality and non-discrimination clauses in the Bill of Rights.

In 2012, I joined the Supreme Court's prestigious clerkship programme alongside four other colleagues.. The Judiciary, under the leadership of former Chief Justice Dr. Willy Mutunga, had embraced a legal research and clerkship system that mirrored practices in the United States legal system. There were five of us, each attached to a Justice of the Court, with a mandate to effectively prepare the Judge for trial and adjudication.

This is where I encountered brilliance of immeasurable proportions. Loise, Prisca, Sam, Shem and I challenged and enriched each other intellectually while working on producing material that supported the Court to develop indigenous jurisprudence, setting the Court's decisions as anchor precedents in comparable jurisdictions in Africa and the Commonwealth. During this time, we participated in judicial dialogues between the Supreme Court of Kenya and Constitutional Courts of India, South Africa, Colombia, and the United Kingdom principally on the role of the Judiciary as a tool to effect checks and balances within the framework of liberal constitutional governance. The Constitution offered me a canvas to exercise my mind and daily life on the values of freedom. It gave me and millions of other Kenyans the confidence to thrive in a country guided by the rule of law.

The Africa We Want Is
"An Africa of good governance, democracy, respect for human rights, justice and the rule of law"
African Union Agenda 2063

There Are No Failures in Life, Only Lessons

Dear Reader,

It is not without struggle that you have found a voice—your own voice. Hesitation and hijacks of doubt have marked the course of your life as they have generations of women before you. Constantly, and with each dawning light, you have shed the fear of justifying your life by showing up, speaking up, and doing things even when fear grips you. You push yourself to do things, even though you are afraid. You know deeply that the energy you bring to the world cannot and must not be depleted by a system that may not value the audacity of a generation rising to its highest power. You know that you must remain grateful, open, conscious and bold enough to push doors that may lead to places that you have never known or imagined. You and your peers, however life's favour has placed you, are joined together in a war to save humanity from self-destruction. That call is an act of justice, solidarity, and a re-enactment of the very basic understanding of human existence. We are all connected by a common duty to empower one another. Beyond status, gender, age, nationality, or any distinguishing features of our realities, we are bound together by nature. May we therefore take each other's struggles as our own. That is the atom of justice.

CHAPTER SEVEN

The Shame of Being Different
by Ms. Yasmine Ouirhrane

"I am Nala because I believe that whatever you want to do, wherever you want to go, you belong there"

I was born in the small city of Biella in northern Italy to a Moroccan father and an Italian mother. Biella is quite a conservative city. My father, a first-generation immigrant, faced a lot because of his different skin color and north-African accent. Because of his experiences, he gave interviews in local newspapers and spoke openly about the need to embrace diversity.

My mother came from an Italian family. When my parents announced their desire to get married, they faced a lot of opposition. At that time in 1990, mixed-raced marriages were not common and were even frowned upon. When some relatives from my mother's side learned about their decision to marry, they cut ties with them. This meant I never got to meet or know some of my relatives. I was only a child and did not understand why we did not visit or know some of my mother's relatives.

My mother was also an immigrant. At the age of six years old, she moved from Sicily in southern Italy to Biella in the North. The economic divide between the north and the south of Italy, in addition to the different dialects spoken, made it difficult for an Italian from the South such as my mother to feel welcome and be accepted in the North. She experienced difficulties throughout her primary school and secondary education, not only because of the language barrier but also thanks to her financial situation. She was only a teenager when she had her first child, my stepbrother Luca, and has had to work in order to sustain her family ever since. Witnessing her strength and determination throughout the years has been of great inspiration to me.

I am the product of these two stories of migration. The quest for inclusion was a key element in my upbringing. Growing up in Biella, I never understood why some teachers treated me differently from other students, starting from misspelling my name when going through the class checklist. It made me feel different and not accepted. I could not fathom the fear of difference and the reluctance towards another culture or language.

I am the youngest sister of three. All three of us attended the same schools. On my first day in middle school, going through the attendance sheet, the teacher called out my last name, looked at me and said, "Oh, another one."

My name was not the only source of shame—which my peers mocked daily. They called me "Honda Jazz" in reference to the car. I was also teased for the way I looked. I was very skinny—a bodily existence I could not change since it was genetic. Still, I felt ashamed. I would wear multiple layers of clothes.

I was bothered. I felt bothered by it all. I became conditioned to care about external judgment. For the longest time, I felt ugly. I was always reminded of the ways in which I was "different," and I felt unaccepted.

In addition to all this, my performance at school qualified as "mediocre." My day-to-day learning experiences were marred by feelings of failure and the inability to feel valued by teachers and educators. This meant I would often spend hours in front of a book and not be able to read or decipher sentences. I became quickly distracted in class and was called a troublemaker. Frustrated, I gave up trying to explain to teachers how I felt.

Turning Stigma into a Strength

My "peculiar" behavior, as I learned and discovered years later, was caused by a deficit of attention. Learning to gain focus in school has been a transforming journey, and it is in continuous progress. Overcoming the feeling of failure and managing to build on my strengths has been the most important shift.

I managed to get to graduation. I am a first-generation graduate in my family. I proved to myself that I can achieve what others perceived as impossible. More importantly, I proved to myself that I can achieve whatever I wish, regardless of the amount of effort it requires.

Today, I want to motivate others to do the same.

My journey was paired with mental health challenges in the quest for self-acceptance and self-confidence. I want other women not to feel ashamed about the hardships they endure. We must normalise asking for help. We need to embrace our different identities and support each other on this journey.

You are truly not alone.

My Story of Migration

In 2011, a financial crisis hit Italy. I was fifteen. My family decided to move to France in search of better opportunities. That moment marked the start of a new becoming: I was an individual engaged in spatial mobility, and it was beyond my parents' migration trajectories, my mother from southern to northern Italy, and my father from Morocco to Italy. I began tracing my own migration trajectory.

I have had many firsts since I arrived in France. The first time I saw black and brown individuals working at an office desk or in a bank, I was surprised. I was compelled by comparative thinking. I could not stop myself from drawing comparisons with Italy. Europe's multiple colonial pasts were reflected in both France and Italy at a spatial, social, and economic level. The imperial colonial legacy lived on. I related the divergence in the racial demography to France's colonial written and unwritten past. France's centuries-long colonial project on the African continent and in the Caribbean islands had produced multiple generations of immigrant descents. On the other hand, my father was considered as a "first generation" migrant in Italy.

We settled in Grenoble, a small city surrounded by the French Alps in the southeast of France. Grenoble was green and at the heart of nature, to the extent that it became known as one of Europe's most environment-friendly cities. Yet, behind the green parks and colorful tramways, Grenoble also hosted some of the deadliest neighborhoods in France, often portrayed in the media as the "Chicago of France."

It was in Grenoble that I discovered the banlieue—underprivileged suburbs mostly populated by second and third generation immigrants. My father avoided moving us into the banlieues. He had heard of several episodes of violence and wanted to protect us at all costs. Little did he know that a year later, at the age of sixteen, I would start volunteering in those same banlieues and meet children and youth with ambitious dreams and potential and artistic aspirations, but only few opportunities to realise them.

It is possible to think that the opportunities might have been available. However, one ought to further consider that lack of information and impostor syndrome might have stood as significant obstacles for these children and youth who did not have mentors to look up to.

Volunteering in French Banlieues

My volunteering experience began when I joined a local NGO through the help of a few friends. I supported the organisation with extra-curricular activities on Saturday mornings. These sessions benefitted children ranging from five to seventeen years old.

NalaFem

One of the most striking things I noticed was the children's playing timetable. I used to see the children I taught around the city playing until very late hours at night. When they came the next day on Saturday mornings for the activities we organised, they often looked tired, with sleepy eyes. They were not getting enough sleep.

At this particular moment, I realised that the problem was structural. The children were imitating their peers, and some of their parents were not able to put in place suitable boundaries.

Living in a banlieue, the people one would see around were often the wrong role models. I saw some of these children play with their bikes in ways that imitated older young men who drove recklessly fast on their scooters all day long around the neighborhood. While debating with friends, I would hear them say, "The French don't like us, we were born here but we are not part of society." They repeatedly spoke about a deep sense of alienation. A glorification of criminality was often portrayed as a pathway to upward social mobility. These views were also reflected in French rap music—an industry that has served as an escape from poverty for some immigrant descents living in banlieues. I listened to and analysed the lyrics to get a better sense of what the youngsters were telling me.

I experienced this new space at the NGO as a teenager myself, and a question ran repeatedly through my mind: how could one break the vicious cycle of poverty that often led to violence? It is this precise question that has become the driver of my activism ever since.

I wanted to change the cycle of poverty, and it had to start by proving to the children and youth that dreams are achievable.

"I champion sustainable cities and communities"
United Nations Sustainable Development Goals

During high school, both in Italy and France, teachers had always downplayed my capabilities, advising me to seek less ambitious careers. This is a reality which continues to happen to people of color, who are "statistically" advised to seek low skilled jobs. I refused to comply with their expectations, and I aimed high. I found a strong confidence within myself to take risks and try. This made a significant difference. I lived with the probability of failing, yet it did not stop me. Once again, I wanted to prove to myself that I could effect this change in my community in France.

One particular teacher had an impact on me. Our long debates during her History and Geopolitics classes shaped my thoughts on geopolitics and the world. She held space for me and saw in me a potential no one else had ever told me about before. In addition, the spiritual journey I went through was deeply transformational. It helped me gain confidence and work hard for my success. I acquired a sense of responsibility, and my desire to bring a positive change to society empowered me to improve my performance at school and gain discipline and focus.

A Quest for Peace

When I was in high school, France was hit by several terrorist attacks from extremists who claimed to be religiously motivated. It was hard to conceive that the same spirituality that helped me find peace was used as an ideology to commit deadly and inhumane acts.

Following these attacks, I felt a sense of injustice due to an increased sense of insecurity and the rise of islamophobia and fear of Muslims in France. This was a topic of discussion in class with teachers and classmates. It motivated me later on to start working towards the prevention of extremism.

I joined meetings focused on peace and security. I wrote an article for the Italian Intelligence Review on the prevention of terrorism in Europe, and I was appointed as an Expert on Peace and Security by the European Union and the African Union. I made the quest for peace a priority in my work.

By the time these aspects of my life unfolded, I had managed to get into one of the most prestigious universities of France, once again by taking risks and being overly ambitious. Here is how it happened:

> While debating in high school one day, a peer said to me, "You should do Sciences Po."
> I remember turning to her and asking. "What is that?"
> It was my last year of high school, the year you choose your future path.

"Sciences Po" was the most prominent Political Sciences university of the country. This memory is funny to recall, mainly because some students had been supported by their parents since their first year of high school in preparation for their entry tests into Sciences Po. Their privilege granted them access. In my case, it was randomly mentioned by a classmate. At the last minute! The applications for the test were due in a few months. But as a risk-taker, I dared to try.

I became among 3% of the students from underprivileged backgrounds to graduate from the "Grandes Ecoles"— France's prestigious universities.

I applied to two of these schools. I was not intimidated to enter rooms filled with hundreds of candidates and take the test. I was surprised to learn that I'd gotten admitted to not one but two of these universities. The little girl who did not even know about these particular universities a few months before now had the choice between two out of the top ten Political Sciences institutions many dreamed of. I attended Sciences Po Bordeaux. This meant moving to the opposite side of France.

I stepped into this new academic space with impostor syndrome —even though getting admitted into university had been the product of hard work and determination. I hid my impostor syndrome with a sense of being overly confident. I will be honest, for the longest time being the only veiled woman in that school meant a continuous self-questioning of my legitimacy. My ambition was my main drive and it accompanied me from day one. I wanted to share it with other youth and advocate for their rights to have a place in national institutions.

At university, I was also confronted by students with a very distinct background from mine. Some had wealthy parents, while others were the offspring of elected politicians or Ambassadors. I was surrounded by classmates who held diverging views on French banlieues, inequalities, and social justice. For instance, I would find myself debating with classmates on topics such as, "Is France a country of equal opportunities?" I would be the only person in the room countering that idea. I saw first-hand what it meant for a child to benefit from free education and get an opportunity to have high-quality studies, but the percentage of students from the working class who broke into these universities was significantly low. I am only one of the few exceptions in a system of structural inequality that prevents access to equal opportunities.

NalaFem

Different lived experiences and different views did not prevent students from exchanging views in a constructive way. My experience, while filled with challenges, was also packed with great opportunities.

While studying in Bordeaux, I continued to volunteer with local NGOs to help children from banlieues with their homework, and in parallel I started engaging internationally. I benefited from a scholarship to study in France, Italy, and California, and I got access to spheres I never thought I could join. Since my very first year in university, I recognised the importance of advocating for the rights of immigrants' sons and daughters. Speaking multiple European languages and having travelled across the continent, my journey took me to the European level.

"I call for economic justice"
Africa Young Women Beijing+25 Manifesto

The Power of Networking

One thing I was not afraid of doing was speaking up, sharing my views, and daring to take the floor. The ability I had to vehiculate my ideas led me to reach places in which I never saw women who look like me, or of my age, speaking.

One of my very first panels was at a United Nations General Assembly (UNGA) side event in 2018 with the Former Prime Minister of Australia, a French Minister of Gender Equality, and a French Ambassador present in the room. It was the very first time I would openly speak about the need for inclusion of young people with immigrant backgrounds in France, while having in front of me French decision-makers.

I was scared. I mentioned the terrorist attacks that divided our country, the fears of citizens, but also the need for more opportunities for immigrant descendants. The Minister was listening while scrolling her tablet. I would end my panel and discover after the panel that she gave me a follow on Twitter.

Social media has been a great tool for amplifying my voice and reaching policymakers, especially at the European level. By always actively tweeting to raise discussions on topics that mattered for me, I gained the attention of ambassadors, political figures, and institutions.

Advocating for Immigrant Descendants

My advocacy work led me to travel to four continents, from Paris to New York, from Nairobi to Doha, from Brussels to Addis Ababa. In each place, I was reminded and got to remind others of the importance of advocating for diversity in multiple spheres of power.

That message, to this day, is founded on my experience volunteering on Saturday mornings in the French suburbs of Grenoble and Bordeaux, where I got to see and learn about the missing lobby for immigrant children.

I first worked helping organise Europe's biggest youth-led political festival at the European Parliament, where I curated activities on the topics of peace and security. This experience helped me join the United Network of Young Peacebuilders and work closely with United Nations entities. I then started taking part in several institutional meetings on topics related to inclusion.

Being appointed as a young expert for the European Union and the African Union, joining panels with Prime Ministers and advising senior European representatives, I recognised that our voices were still underrepresented and not given the importance they deserved.

As my voice became heard, I continued to mention the many stories that were still not told. However, in some contexts I would feel tokenised by virtue of being the youngest person and the only person of color invited to speak. I never missed the opportunity to ask for more chairs to be added to the decision-making table and for a meaningful engagement that would not only result in more promises. I wanted to see concrete actions.

Facing Hate Across Europe as an Immigrant Descendant

In 2019, my efforts for inclusion were recognised by the Schwarzkopf Foundation, declaring me "Young European of the Year 2019" for my efforts to promote gender equality and social justice. This was an award for years of work that I got to cherish for a full two days before it made me the target of the far right in France, which sent hundreds of messages of hate and threats my way.

The personal is political. I was targeted for my personal life and choices. I used to wear a hijab and I became the target of online trolls and politicians, including the French Presidential Candidate Marine Le Pen who tweeted about me.

Tragically, the day the Leader of the French far right used my picture to call for votes, I was at Adam's funeral, a seventeen-year-old boy who died while fleeing the police in my city, Grenoble. His life and murder continue to remind me of the importance of my work as an activist and advocate, both against hateful narratives and for the improvement of social conditions of minorities in Europe.

My message bothered racist people, and that is exactly why it was needed and important. This realisation pushed me to move forward despite the threats and insults I received. Though the threats impacted me mentally, I continued to speak up and raise my voice.

Ultimately, this story makes me who I am today, and it is far from being unique. I met dozens of young people in Europe who yearn to be heard as much as I do. They face similar, if not slightly different challenges to mine back when I started out without a platform. I often wonder if what made the difference was my ability to dare, to stand up and take risks so that I may raise my voice and reach places where stories like mine are not heard enough.

This award that caused me much hardship is not only mine. It is a symbolic recognition for all those who look or are perceived differently, those who share common experiences with other immigrant sons and daughters all over Europe and who need to be acknowledged.

Today, I am committed to champion the rights of youth, women, and minorities. I want them to feel ambitious, valued, and included in decision-making processes. Where people see differences, I see bridges and potential waiting to be cultivated; where people see obstacles, I see opportunity to bring change; where people see challenges, I see solutions for a prosperous and inclusive society.

The Africa We Want Is
"An African whose development is people-drive, relying on the
potential offered by the African people, especially its women
and youth, and caring for children"
African Union Agenda 2063

My goal is to reshape our spaces and affirm our right to exist in society. I also want to foster the ambition that young people, particularly girls, need in order to DARE. It is on this quest for representation, and in response to the hate I faced, that I co-founded We Belong, a platform and podcast for the New Daughters of Europe, immigrant descendants.

I started We Belong with Jana Degrott, one of the youngest elected politicians in Europe, and Sumaia Saiboub, a talented content creator from Italy. Being part of this project has been a healing process for me. I was part of a support system of people who faced similar challenges to mine in their work. Together we embarked on a journey to share more positive narratives and inspire the next generation with role models we ourselves did not have when we started.

Through our podcast, we have interviewed dozens of women from more than fifteen European countries and from varied backgrounds. Among my favorites, I recall interviewing the football star Nadia Nadim, who came to Europe as an Afghan refugee and ended up playing for the Danish National Team. Her story inspires both power and hope.

Another story I deeply connected with was the one of Fatima Zaman, especially as she later became a close friend and a strategic advisor at We Belong. Fatima witnessed the 7/7 London bombings as a teenager. This motivated her to work as a counter-extremist beside the late Kofi Annan. She is one of my main inspirations today. Additionally, I learned volumes from an interview with Samira Rafaela, a Member of the European Parliament from The Netherlands. Her presence in this institution is very much needed and I hope that through her story other young women will be encouraged to run for office.

While we want to foster ambition and give a sense of confidence to young women, we also use social media campaigns to bring deeper reflections on diversity in society. One of our campaigns focused on "What does it mean to be European to you?" Dozens of contributors shared their stories, challenges, and hopes to feel and be seen as European as immigrant descendants. We want to turn this challenge into a strength and continue to advocate for more representation in all spheres of power. When you can see it, it is easier to believe that it is possible.

We want to ensure that diversity is celebrated as a strength. Our core message is: whatever you want to do, you belong there!

Acknowledgments

We are proud to introduce *I am Nala*, the first published book by Nala Feminist Collective as the result of tireless work of the auhtors, the editors and the NalaFEM team. We acknowledge the valuable contributions of the authors, namely Ms. Aya Chebbi (Tunisia), Ms. Bogolo Joy Kenewendo (Botswana), Ms. Martine Kessy Ekomo Soignet (Central African Republic), Ms. Oluwaseun Ayodeji Osowobi (Nigeria), Ms. Rosebell Kagumire (Uganda), Ms. Rose Wachuka Macharia (Kenya), and Ms. Yasmine Ouirhrane (Italy). We are grateful for the generous support of the editing committee, namely Dr. Novuyo Tshuma, the lead editor of the book for her commitment and guidance throughout the process, Ms. Amina Alaoui Soulimani, Dr. Syeda Re'em Hussain, Ms. Rahel Weldeab Sebhatu, and Ms. Soraya Addi, the support editors for their continued support to the authors throughout their writing journeys.

We thank Dr. Natalia Kanem, Executive Director of UNFPA, and Dr. Ameenah Gurib-Fakim, Former President of Mauritius for honoring our invitation to include their strong voices to this book in support of young women and girls from Africa and the Diaspora. We appreciate the generous support of the Rockefeller Foundation in the publishing of this book.

NalaFEM is grateful to those who provided support and guidance in bringing this book to life and we are proud to highlight that this book is women-led and Africa-led.

About the Authors

Aya Chebbi

Aya Chebbi is the founder and chair of Nala Feminist Collective. She is a multi award-winning Pan-African feminist. She served as the first ever African Union Special Envoy on Youth and the youngest diplomat at the African Union Commission Chairperson's Cabinet (2018-2021). Prior to this role, she rose to prominence as a voice for democracy and a political activist during 2010/2011 Tunisia's Revolution.

Over the span of the past decade, she has single-handedly transformed the youth participation space across Africa and created various online and offline platforms with a holistic focus on youth and women leadership. From running an award-winning blog Proudly Tunisian and a popular Mentorship Programme Y-PHEM to building Afrika Youth Movement, one of Africa's largest pan-African youth-led movements and Afresist, a think tank documenting youth work in Africa.

She served on the Board of Directors of CIVICUS, World Refugee Council, Oxfam Independent Commission on Sexual Misconduct, Independent Panel for Pandemic Preparedness and Response among others. She is a graduate of University of Tunis El Manar with Bachelor's in International Relations, Fulbright scholar at Georgia Southern University and Mo Ibrahim Foundation Scholar for her Masters in African Politics at SOAS, University of London. She received the 2019 Gates Foundation Campaign Award and was named in Forbes' Africa's 50 Most Powerful Women.

NalaFem

Bogolo J. Kenewendo

Bogolo J. Kenewendo is a global economist with deep expertise in international trade and development. She has a particular focus on Pan-African development and a passion for accelerating digitization and innovation across the continent. As the Minister of Investment, Trade and Industry in Botswana, she implemented reforms to significantly improve the ease of doing business, open up both domestic and international markets, and position the country to succeed in the global value chains as well as the digital economy. During her tenure, she was the youngest Cabinet Minister in Africa and in Botswana's History.

Kenewendo is also a vocal advocate for gender equity and protection of children's rights. She has received global recognition for her work, being appointed as a member of the G7 Gender Equality Advisory Council, Senior Africa Advisor to Jack Ma Foundation and Africa Business Heroes, Jury for the FAO Africa Innovation Prize, a member of United Nations Secretary-General António Guterres' High-Level Panel on Digital Cooperation and group on Financing for Development, a member of the World Economic Forum (WEF) Global Future Council on Global Public Goods in the Fourth Industrial Revolution, WEF Trade Action Group and a WEF Young Global Leader.

She currently serves as Managing Director of Kenewendo Advisory, a Non-resident Fellow at Center for Global Development and sits on multiple corporate boards.

Martine Kessy Ekomo Soignet

Kessy Martine Ekomo-Soignet, holds a Master 2 in Geo-Politics, International Security and Sociology. She is a recognized expert who contributes to various journals and research on development and peace and security issues and more specifically on youth and civil society in Africa. She is a community leader and founder of the national NGO URU (2014), working for effective youth participation in the peace and recovery process in the Central African Republic.

In 2016, she was appointed by the Secretary-General of the United Nations as an expert for the Progress Study on the Youth, Peace and Security Agenda, in accordance with UN Security Council Resolution 2250 (Youth, Peace and Security). Since then, she has been a member of the Global Coalition on Youth, Peace and Security. She briefed the Security Council and the UN General Assembly on the urgency of strengthening efforts to help young people contribute effectively to the resolution and prevention of conflicts around the world.

In 2021, she created the consulting firm Peace and Development Watch Central African Republic specializing in prospective analysis and project evaluation. It includes an observatory that gives the population a voice on major national challenges as well as a center for stimulating entrepreneurship. She represents PeaceDirect and sits as Board Member of the organization in the UK. Kessy is also a Board member of iDove, an African Union initiative that aims to raise awareness among youth about issues related to radicalization and violent extremism.

Oluwaseun Ayodeji Osowobi

Oluwaseun Ayodeji Osowobi leads national advocacy to achieve SDGs 3, 5 and 16 in Nigeria by deploying effective solutions to challenge systemic social barriers that promote social injustices and limit access to justice and health services for survivors of sexual and gender-based violence (SGBV). As a survivor of sexual violence, Oluwaseun Ayodeji founded Stand to End Rape Initiative (STER), a leading youth-led organisation that adopts a comprehensive approach of working with communities to generate sustainable homegrown solutions and partners with local and national groups on systems-level prevention and intervention to respond to the dearth of available resources to support SGBV survivors. STER provides access to justice for survivors with holistic services such as general advice, legal aid and representation, medical support, and psychosocial and health services empowerment in an impartial and non-discriminatory way.

In seven (7) years, Oluwaseun has fostered systemic change through educational programs, provided capacity-building on SGBV prevention and intervention to state institutions, and supported policy advocacy to enjoin the government to pass gender-centred Laws. In 2019, she collaborated with partners to establish Nigeria's first national Sex Offenders Register and collaborated on the BBC Sex for Grades documentary to push an anti-sexual harassment policy. In honour of her work, Oluwaseun was named the Commonwealth Young Person for the Year 2019, a TIME 100 NEXT Honouree and awarded the 2020 Global Citizen Prize: Nigeria's Hero. Recently, she won the 2022 United States International Visitors Leadership Program Impact Award. She is a founding member of the Feminist Coalition and Council member of Nala Feminist Collective.

Rosebell Kagumire

Rosebell Kagumire (She/Her) is a writer and editor at African Feminism. She is a Pan-African feminist activist who works at the intersection of media, gender and development. She recently co-edited a book: Challenging Patriarchy: The Role of Patriarchy in the Roll-Back of Democracy. She was honored with the Anna Guèye 2018 award for her contribution to digital democracy, justice and equality on the African continent by Africtivistes, a network of African activists for democracy. She holds a Masters degree in Media, Peace and Conflict Studies from the UN-mandated University of Peace in Costa Rica. She has done short term studies in nonviolent conflict at the Fletcher School and Global Leadership and Public Policy at the Harvard Kennedy School. Her undergraduate degree is in Mass Communication from Makerere University, Uganda.

Rose Wachuka Macharia

Rose Wachuka Macharia is the first female and youngest Chief of Staff to the Chief Justice and President of the Supreme Court of Kenya Hon. Justice Martha K. Koome, EBS. Since her appointment in July 2021, she has led the development of the *Social Transformation through Access to Justice* Vision of the Chief Justice to the Judiciary and is charged with the responsibility of developing an implementation mechanism to deliver its promise to the Kenyan people. The Vision completes the social justice promise of the Constitution of Kenya by providing expanded avenues to deliver access to justice, enhanced accountability, seamless inter-agency collaboration and shared leadership. It has been lauded by practitioners and the international community as the most impacting Vision of the Judiciary in history. Rose is also leading a team to develop the third Blueprint of the Judiciary to guide the third phase of Judicial reforms and transformation. Rose is an Oxford-trained Advocate of the High Court of Kenya who has rendered distinguished legal practice for the past decade. She has also dedicated half of her life to international and national assignments geared towards pursuit of access to justice.

Yasmine Ouirhrane

Yasmine Ouirhrane is the co-founder of We Belong, a platform and podcast that amplifies the voice of the New Daughters of Europe, immigrant descents. Since the age of 16, she volunteered in underprivileged neighborhoods of France to foster social inclusion. In a quest to advocate for inclusive leadership, she also served as an appointed expert for the European Union and the African Union and she delivered dozens of recommendations to international institutions, including the European Commission, Foreign Affairs Canada and Wilton Park UK Foreign Office. She provided workshops on access to education, equal opportunities and social entrepreneurship for Tony Blair Institute, Change.org and EM Business School, among others. She was recognised as Young European of the Year 2019 by the Schwarzkopf Foundation, EDD Young Leader by the European Commission, Women Deliver Young Leader and she served as a member of the Gender Innovation Agora at UN Women Arabic. Yasmine currently works in the tech business sector and she is passionate about the intersection between innovation and social change.

Printed in the United States
by Baker & Taylor Publisher Services